Salad Plants

for your vegetable garden

By

ROGER PHILLIPS
& MARTYN RIX

Research by Nicky Foy
Design Gill Stokoe, Jill Bryan & Debby Curry

A Pan Original

Acknowledgements

We would like to thank the following gardens and suppliers for allowing us to visit them and photograph their plants:
The Royal Horticultural Society's garden at Wisley for numerous specimens from the model vegetable garden; Barnsley House; Ryton Organic Garden; NIAB, Cambridge; Sandling Park; The Ballymaloe Cookery School Garden; Leiden Botanic Garden; Villandry; Green Gulch Farm, California.
The following also helped us by allowing us to take photographs in their gardens, and in other ways:
Rosemary Verey, Joy Larkcom, Marilyn Inglis, Colin Martin, Anne Thatcher, Leslie Land and Anthony Rix.

First published 1998 by Pan
an imprint of Macmillan Publishers Limited
25 Eccleston Place, London SW1W 9NF
and Basingstoke
Associated companies throughout the world
ISBN 0-330-35551-1
Copyright in the text and illustrations
© Roger Phillips and Martyn Rix
The right of the authors to be identified as the authors
of this work has been asserted by them in accordance with the Copyright, Designs and Patents Act 1988.

Colour Reproduction by Aylesbury Studios Ltd.
Printed by Butler and Tanner Ltd. Frome, Somerset

Contents

Introduction

It used to be that the word 'salad' conjured up three images: tomato, lettuce and cucumber, at least in Britain, Europe and much of North America. But over the last 10–15 years the notion of what constitutes a 'salad' has changed dramatically. No longer does salad mean a few wilting lettuce leaves adorned with some slices of tomato and cucumber; nowadays it means as wide a variety of vegetables as one has the imagination and creativity to combine together. Herbs, spices and salad greens from all over the world are now widely available and with them has come a host of new ideas about how to put them together in interesting and delicious combinations.

The purpose of this book is to present the keen amateur gardener-cum-gourmet with an interesting and fairly comprehensive selection of salad plants that can quite easily be grown in the garden and herb garden or, in many cases, in pots or on windowsills. We have tried to include most of the traditional favourite salad plants such as tomatoes and carrots, lettuces and spring onions but we have also included many plants that have only become internationally fashionable in the last decade or so, such as rocket, Chinese spinach, coriander and the edible flowers.

The Text

The plants are divided into five sections: leaves, roots and sprouts, fruits and beans, herbs and flowers although there is, of course, some overlap where, for example, both the young leaves of a plant and its roots can be eaten, such as celery, or flowers and young fruit as in courgettes. We have attempted to keep the text simple, avoiding complicated botanical or horticultural terms if possible. Each entry gives the main facts about the plant and, in the 'Planting Help', advice on how to grow it.

Growing Salad Plants

There are no hard and fast rules about growing salad plants except perhaps that they always need to have plenty of water if they are to thrive. The plants in this book

have basically been selected with gardeners throughout northern Europe and North America in mind. However, differences in climate will mean that there will be slightly different requirements with regard to protection from extremes of temperature, time of sowing, harvesting and so on. For this reason we have not given temperature zones to individual plants. The general principle is that many salads will overwinter in mild climates (US zones 7–11) and many, such as lettuces, may grow better through the mild days from autumn to spring, whereas in colder climates the same varieties can be grown through the summer.

This book does not set out to be a manual for the cultivation of salad plants but we have provided brief notes on cultivation, mainly based on our own experience, which should be enough for amateurs to grow a reasonable crop. Different plants require and use up different nutrients; however the use of ample organic manure is fundamental to the success of most salad plants and especially those grown on sandy or clay soils. Organic matter provides food for plants, especially nitrogen and phosphate; it improves sandy and light, chalky soils, because the humus holds more water and makes clay soils more easily workable. Organic matter for vegetables is traditionally provided by mixing cow manure with straw, but household and garden compost heaps are other good sources of humus and plant food, as are horse manure and leaf mould. Compost-making bins are useful for making small amounts of compost in a short time.

The Potager at Barnsley House

The Potager at Barnsley House

'Rhubarb Chard' growing among herbs

Propagation

Most salad plants are grown from seed. One question must first be settled; do we plant the seeds straight into the garden, or do we start them in pots or trays in a greenhouse or frame and put out the small plants? Starting the plants indoors has many advantages; the young seedlings are less likely to be damaged by cold weather, slugs or bugs; the young plants can be spaced correctly and will not need thinning, so that precious seed is not wasted, and in small areas better use can be made of the space available. Many nurseries now sell young plants, especially young Brassicas, and this is an easier way of ensuring a good crop.

Most plants can be easily transplanted as seedlings. There are only a few instances of plants which do not survive being transplanted; these include carrots, radishes

Spring onions and celtuce in a market near Dali

and other root crops in which the seedling makes a long taproot at an early stage. These need to be planted in position from seed and then thinned.

so in dry areas plant leafy vegetables in depressions which can be watered easily. Generally a strong-growing healthy plant is less affected by disease than a weak one.

Pests and Diseases

The best way to prevent damage from diseases and pests is to deal with the problem at the very first sign of infection. Most people will not want to spray complex poisons onto their salad vegetables. Aphids and caterpillars may be controlled with a spray of soapy water and many leaf fungi can be controlled with a combination of copper sulphate and lime. Powdery mildews are worst on plants which have become dry at the root,

Rose petals are a pretty addition to salads

7

Savoy cabbages at Sandling Park

'Hispi'   'Castello'   'Mohrenkopf' (*left*) and 'Vesta'

Cabbages

Cabbages or *brassicas* are an enormous group of plants that have been cultivated for about 3000 years. The first reference to them being eaten was found in Greek literature in 600 BC. Native to N Europe and the Mediterranean, cabbages grow wild on chalk and limestone sea cliffs, often near towns and villages, or associated with colonies of breeding gulls.

Modern cabbages are believed to have been developed first in Germany where both red and white varieties have been grown since 1150. Today, there are eight main types of cabbages: Spring, Summer, Autumn, Savoy, Savoy Hybrids, January King, White Winter and Red. Almost all varieties can be eaten either raw (if shredded finely enough), steamed or stir-fried, but generally the leafy dark-leaved Spring and Summer types can be a little bitter raw and are better cooked, while the dense-hearted White Winter and Red cabbages are ideal for winter salads, particularly if combined with grated carrots, nuts and sultanas.

PLANTING HELP   Cabbages grow best in well-drained, fertile chalky soil in an open position with plenty of light. The seed should be sown in trays or blocks, or singly in pots and then planted out when 1–2 months old. The soil should be cleared but not dug-over before planting to give better anchorage. The size of the heads will be determined by how closely the young plants are spaced; 14in (35cm) apart for small heads, 18in (45cm) apart for large ones. To avoid the problem of 'toppling' in light soils, plant the cabbages in furrows about 4in (10cm) deep and then fill them in as the plants grow; on windy sites and with tall varieties you may find it necessary to stake the plants. Give cabbages plenty of moisture until they reach maturity.

Pests can be a problem. The worst is cabbage root fly which causes yellowing of the outer leaves and wilting in hot weather. To avoid attack, place a barrier, such as roofing felt, around the base of the plant, covering the soil for about 4in (10cm) around. Other pests and diseases to look out for are clubroot, large and small white butterflies, mealy aphids and cabbage whites.

'Hispi'   An F$_I$ hybrid that grows to 10in (25cm) tall with pointed heads up to 7in (18cm) in diameter. It should be sown indoors early and then planted out to mature rapidly in late spring. This variety is particularly suitable for summer salads. 'Kingspi' is similar.

'Castello'   An F$_I$ hybrid with good standing ability, this is an early to mid-season autumn cabbage with a dense round head and grey green leaves. It takes 80 days to mature from transplanting.

'January King', 'Pontoise', 'Blaugrüner', 'Winter', 'Chou Milan de l'Hermitage'   An old French variety listed in 1883 and now a group of varieties, this is very hardy when planted in early July. These cultivars mature by early winter, often standing through the winter. They have slightly crinkly, purplish leaves and an excellent flavour.

'Mohrenkopf', 'Negrohead'   An old variety known since 1911, it grows to 20in (50cm) tall and has a dense, round purple head up to 8in (20cm) across. 'Red Dutch' is very similar and is the variety often found in seed catalogues.

'Pixie'   This grows to 9in (23cm) tall with a small solid head to 6in (15cm) in diameter. Sow in autumn to mature in late spring for both spring greens and hearts. This variety is suitable for those with small gardens.

'Vesta'   A red cabbage that is suitable for storage.

'Pixie'

'January King'

9

KALE

Curly kale 'Frosty'; the young leaves are good in salads

Kales

Kales were probably the earliest type of cultivated brassicas, being similar to the wild forms of *Brassica oleracea*. Most kales have a tall thick stem and are very hardy, overwintering and being harvested in spring when the young leaves and shoots develop. Kale can be grown for either ornamental or culinary use.

The ornamental varieties are at their best in the winter months, developing their striking purple, pink, white, grey and green colours after the temperatures drop to 15°F (−10°C); their colourful frilly or serrated leaves look extremely pretty in the garden. Many of the kales grown as culinary varieties have very crisped and curled leaves and, though they look attractive, are considered to be too coarse for eating in salads, so are best steamed or stir-fried. However, the youngest leaves of the dwarf variety 'Frosty' can be used in salads.

PLANTING HELP   Kale seed is sown in May and the plants are set out in July in soil that has been prepared with plenty of organic matter. The dwarf varieties should be planted 18in (45cm) apart and the larger ones 2½ft (75cm) apart. If you want an early crop of young greens, sow seed thickly under glass in January or February and when the young plants are 6in (15cm) high, cut like spinach. The plants will resprout.

'Frosty'   A dwarf curly kale that grows to 12in (30cm) and is excellent in salads.

'Palm Tree cabbage', an ornamental variety

Calabrese 'Shogun'

'Palm Tree Cabbage', **'Chou Palmier'**   An old variety of kale, known since the 19th century; it has narrow, recurved, savoyed leaves in a rosette on top of the stem. 'Nero di Toscana' from Italy, is very similar.

Broccoli

Reputed to have originated from Italy, Crete, Cyprus and the eastern Mediterranean in the 17th century, from where it spread to northern Europe, broccoli is referred to as 'Italian Asparagus' in Miller's *Gardener's Dictionary* of 1724.

There are three main types of broccoli: Annual broccoli, which matures in the summer and is generally green or occasionally purple and is commonly known as Calabrese; Romanesco broccoli, which matures in late summer or autumn and has numerous yellowish green conical groups of buds arranged in spirals; and Sprouting broccoli, which is an overwintering white or purple annual or perennial that is ready in early spring. There is also an old variety called Perennial broccoli which is still available, generally known as 'Nine Star'.

Romanesco 'Minaret'

PLANTING HELP   Calabrese and Romanesco can be sown where they are to grow, in threes, 8in (20cm) apart in rows. The seedlings should then be thinned to a single plant and given plenty of water so that they can grow on as fast as possible. Romanesco can be used throughout the winter if the plants are protected from wind and rain by a frame. Sprouting and Perennial broccolis should be sown in a seed bed in late spring and the young plants transplanted 24in (60cm) apart about 8 weeks later. Soil should be well drained and not too nitrogen-rich, otherwise the plants get sappy and too leafy. The aim should be to bring on the hardiest plants so that they are not killed by a cold winter. Lightly steamed broccoli is delicious when eaten cold with a vinaigrette dressing.

Broccoli 'Early White Sprouting'

'Early Purple Sprouting'   A very traditional variety of broccoli which you can begin to crop in early spring (according to the season) and continue to pick into late spring with smaller and smaller shoots.

'Early White Sprouting'   The white equivalent to 'Early Purple Sprouting'.

'Minaret'   A Romanesco-type broccoli in which the greenish heads are divided into pointed groups of florets. This variety is suitable for sowing in late spring and harvesting in the autumn or, if protected, until winter.

'Shogun'   A Calabrese with tall stalks and bluish grey central heads up to 4in (10cm) across on narrow stems. It is tolerant of wet weather and suitable for sowing indoors in autumn and kept under cover for an early crop in early summer.

Broccoli 'Early Purple Sprouting'

'Kasumi'

'Eskimo' *(in the centre of the picture)*

Chinese Leaves

Chinese leaves or Chinese cabbage are like large Cos lettuce or cabbage with a crisp, watery texture and mustard-like taste. Also known as Celery cabbage, Pe Tsai and Peking cabbage, there are many varieties and a great deal of confusion about the names of the different species. The main categories are the solid-headed varieties, which can be both round and elongated (Chinese leaves) and the open leafy varieties with broad stalks such as Pak Choi.

In China, Chinese leaves are known as 'Yellow tooth radish' and used extensively in cooking for their succulent texture either braised, boiled, steamed or stir-fried. They keep well and the Chinese often hang them for a few days, believing that they are sweeter when wilted. The heart and crisp leaves can be used in salads or boiled in soup, while the leaves can be blanched and filled with a fresh shrimp or minced pork stuffing. The mild yet pungent flavour makes it a good accompaniment to both delicate and rich dishes.

'Eskimo' An F_I hybrid, this unusual variety has a self-blanching heart of creamy white leaves.

'Kasumi' This round variety has dense, heavy heads with a short internal stalk and good resistance to bolting.

'Joi Choi' An F_I hybrid, this plant has very white leaf stalks.

'Mei Quing Pak Choi' Another F_I hybrid, this has a green leaf stalk and good resistance to bolting.

'Joi Choi'

CHINESE LEAVES

A vegetable garden in Chengdu, Sichuan, China

'Mei Quing Pak Choi'

'Early Jade Pagoda'

'Tat Soi', a very hardy vatiety

CHINESE LEAVES

'Jade Pagoda'

Pak Choi

'Jade Pagoda' An F1 hybrid that grows up to 14in (35cm) tall and 6in (15cm) across, it has dark green loose heads with a long internal stalk and good resistance to bolting.

'Early Jade Pagoda' This is a quick-maturing form of 'Jade Pagoda'.

'Tat Soi' *Brassica rapa* var. *rosularis* This variety has very dark green, spoon-shaped leaves in a perfect rosette. The blades are usually pressed flat on the ground but sometimes the leaves are more upright. A very hardy plant that can survive both frost and snow.

Pak Choi *Brassica rapa* var. *chinensis* A small fast-growing annual with a rosette of bright green, veined leaves with thick white stems. Some varieties do well in hot temperatures, maturing in as little as five weeks; others prefer cooler climates and grow more slowly. Cook quickly in water or stir-fry in oil for only a couple of minutes to prevent the leaves becoming tough and turning an unpleasant khaki green.

PLANTING HELP Varieties grown as young greens or small flowering plants, such as Pak Choi, are easy to grow, only needing rich soil, plenty of water and warm temperatures. They should be sown in midsummer so that they are ready to crop about five weeks later. Generally robust, they are not too prone to pests and diseases.

Chinese cabbage with its dense, white, crunchy heart is not so easy to grow. Fertile soil, warm temperatures and regular watering – as much as 5 gallons (22 litres) a day – are required for it to grow quickly. It is best planted from early to late summer to crop from autumn to winter. If planted in the spring there is the risk of the plant failing to grow a heart if there is a sudden drop in temperature. However, if it is grown under cover in a cold frame or unheated greenhouse, Chinese cabbage can be used as a cut-and-come-again salad for much of the winter. Like cabbage it is prone to pests and diseases such as clubroot, cabbage root fly, aphids and mildew and the thin leaves can easily be damaged by slugs.

Watercress beds in Hampshire, where chalk srteams provide the perfect growing conditions

Watercress

Watercress

A hardy perennial herb native to Europe, North Africa and Asia, *Nasturtium officinale* is now abundant throughout the world. It is commonly found growing wild in shallow, slow-moving water in rivers, streams and ditches. Its specific name indicates that it was formerly included in lists of medicinal plants and it is recorded in Dioscorides' *Materia medica* of 77 AD. Watercress has been recognized as an important salad plant since Roman times, for its pungent flavour and as a source of vitamin C and minerals to protect against scurvy. It has also been considered an effective hair tonic to promote the growth of thick hair when used externally, and juice from the crushed leaves was recommended by Culpeper for clearing the complexion of blemishes, spots and freckles. Valued for its pungent flavour, it is commonly used in salads, stir-fries and soups.

Care should be taken when picking it in the wild because of the possibility of liver fluke infestation, which can easily occur if cattle or sheep are grazed anywhere near water that flows into the area in which watercress grows.

PLANTING HELP   Watercress is not often grown by amateurs because of the specialized conditions it requires. Gardens with a chalk or limestone spring or a pure stream running at a constant temperature of about 50°F (10°C) and plenty of dappled shade are the optimum conditions, and if you have them, you should plant young rooted pieces of watercress about 6in (15cm) apart in the soil along the edges of the stream in spring. You can also try growing small amounts of watercress in pots. Put some rooted pieces of watercress in a pot which has a layer of gravel at the bottom and is filled with rich potting soil mixed with a little fresh limestone. Stand the pot in a dish of cool water and change it every day. Keep it in a sheltered spot that has plenty of light, add good compost every now and then and snip off any flowering shoots.

taproot and a smooth branching stem that grows 1–3ft (30–90cm) tall. The leaves are smooth, glossy and dark green with toothed or wavy margins. The generic name comes from the fact that it was the only green plant that could be gathered on St Barbara's Day, the 4th of December. It has been eaten for centuries as a salad or pot herb and was popular with early settlers who introduced it to North America. It also makes a delicious vegetable lightly steamed or boiled and served with butter.

Land Cress

Land Cress

A hardy biennial herb, Land Cress or American Winter Cress, *Barbarea verna* is native to the western Mediterranean region and widely naturalized in much of C and W Europe, North America, South Africa, Japan and New Zealand. Land Cress has a yellow taproot and erect, generally branching stems that grow 8–18in (20–45cm) tall. The rosette leaves are deeply divided, dark green and glossy and have a hot spicy flavour that is delicious in salads.

PLANTING HELP   Land Cress is easy to grow from seed. It thrives best in moist, humus-rich soil and should be planted either in early spring for a summer crop or in mid- to late summer for an autumn crop that will last until the following spring. Seeds usually germinate more reliably if planted in seed boxes. When ready for transplanting, space the seedlings 8in (20cm) apart and keep well watered until firmly established. Crop the small central leaves first, or cut the whole head above ground level – more leaves will grow.

Winter Cress

A biennial or perennial herb similar in flavour to watercress, Winter Cress or Yellow Rocket, *Barbarea vulgaris* is native to Europe and North Africa, and naturalized in North America, New Zealand and Australia. It has a stout yellowish

PLANTING HELP   To encourage more leaf growth remove the flowering stems as they appear and pick the outer leaves as the plant regrows.

Winter Cress

Rocket flowering in a garden on the Isle of Mull

Rocket

An annual or overwintering herb also known as Arugula, Roquette, Rucola, *Eruca sativa* (syn. *Eruca vesicaria*) is native to the Mediterranean and E Asia and naturalized in other parts of Europe and in North America. It is found growing in waste places and cultivated in herb gardens. Rocket is a strong-smelling plant with a slender taproot and hairy stem that grows to 3½ft (1m) tall. The deeply lobed leaves are lyre-shaped and toothed. Rocket has a long history of cultivation in Europe both as a salad and as a medicinal plant.

In recent years it has become very popular in Europe and America as a salad vegetable. The pungent, peppery taste of the young leaves adds interest to milder salads, and it is frequently served with tomatoes and mozzarella cheese or shavings of parmesan as an hors d'œuvre. Rocket can also be lightly cooked like spinach and served as a vegetable. It is reputed to be an excellent tonic and the oil extracted from the seeds was said to be an aphrodisiac.

PLANTING HELP   Rocket can be grown from seed in any soil, in a sunny position, in spring or early autumn in mild areas where the plants can survive over winter. After 30 days the leaves are ready to be cut and eaten as required. Pinch off the buds to prevent it flowering as flowers can cause the leaves to become bitter. It will also grow happily in a pot.

Rocket

Lamb's Lettuce

Also called Corn Salad, Fetticus, Nüsslisalad, Mâche. There are about 30 species of these hardy low-growing annuals. *Valerianella locusta* is native to Europe from Britain to Turkey, and cultivated in Europe for centuries. , there are over 15 varieties available in the US. It is very commonly eaten when young as a salad in Europe. Its mild tender leaves have a slightly nutty flavour which makes a delicious addition to salads in winter and early spring.

PLANTING HELP   Lamb's lettuce can be grown easily from seed in most soils and conditions. Either plant directly into the ground or sow in seed boxes and transplant the young seedlings. It is a slow-growing plant taking up to three months to reach maturity, but it can be used as a cut-and-come-again crop at the seedling stage, or the whole head can be cut to within an inch of the ground when mature and fresh growth will be made. Sow in late summer for an autumn or winter crop or in autumn for transplanting under cover in the early winter. This will give a crop during the winter and new growth will also be made in the spring. If crops are left out in the winter they will survive surprisingly low temperatures but their quality and flavour will be better if they are protected by cloches. *Valerianella eriocarpa* is a more southerly species very commonly grown in Italy (*not illustrated*).

Lamb's lettuce

Dandelion

A hardy perennial native throughout the Northern Hemisphere, *Taraxacum officinale* is commonly found growing wild in pastures, lawns, roadsides and in gardens where it is regarded as a weed. Dandelion or Pissenlit, as it is sometimes called, has a fleshy root and a simple, hollow flowering stem that grows 4–8in (10–20cm) tall. The leaves are lance-shaped forming a rosette. Used for centuries, the curative properties of dandelions have been known, as a tonic, purifier, diuretic and aid to digestion. However, as well as being an active medicinal herb, it is a wholesome food. The young leaves are delicious in soups or salads; the French *salade de pissenlits* uses the young leaves tossed in a vinaigrette with bits of warm crisp bacon and croutons. The flowers and leaves can be made into dandelion wine and the roasted and ground roots are a coffee substitute. Blanched leaves can be cooked like spinach and eaten as a vegetable. In France, various cultivars have been selected and are grown in gardens and blanched like endive to make them tender and less bitter.

Dandelion flowers

PLANTING HELP   Dandelions can be grown in most soils and conditions, but they do not like to become waterlogged. Seeds should be sown in spring or early summer, either in seed boxes for later transplanting or *in situ* to be thinned out later to about 14in (35cm) apart. In late summer, blanch a few plants at a time. This can be done outside in mild areas or inside where winters are cold. After using the blanched leaves the plants should be discarded. Remember that the roots go very deep and are not easy to remove.

Chinese spinach

Chinese spinach with Lemon Grass, in Sichuan

Houttuynia

Houttuynia

A creeping perennial, *Houttuynia cordata* is common in damp woodland in most of temperate E Asia. In China the young leaves and shoots are picked in early spring when they are about 3in (8cm) long, for use in salads or as a cooked vegetable. Three forms of *Houttuynia* are grown in Europe as ornamentals: the wild single form; the double form; and a variegated form with beautiful red and white markings on the leaves. The whole plant has a characteristic ginger-like aromatic flavour.

PLANTING HELP   Houttuynia is easy to grow. It prefers moist soil and partial shade and forms loose mats of heart-shaped leaves.

Chinese Spinach

Very similar to spinach, *Amaranthus gangeticus* (syn. *Amaranthus tricolor*) or Chinese Spinach has been grown throughout Asia for centuries. The whole plant is edible although the young leaves and shoots are considered most choice due to their mild but distinct flavour. The Chinese use this vegetable as Westerners use spinach: in soups,

Ice Plant

New Zealand spinach

stir-fries or as a cooked side dish. It can be boiled, steamed, stir-fried or baked.

PLANTING HELP   Chinese spinach is a tropical plant and easy to grow providing there is enough heat and moisture and the soil is very fertile. When grown as a substitute for spinach, the plants should be spaced or thinned to 3–4in (8–10cm) apart and harvested after six to eight weeks when they are about 8in (20cm) tall.

New Zealand Spinach

A perennial plant native to New Zealand, Tasmania and S Australia, China, Japan and southern South America, New Zealand spinach, *Tetragonia tetragonioides* (syn. *Tetragonia expansa*) grows wild on shady and stony beaches along the coast. It was brought to Europe from New Zealand by Sir Joseph Banks in 1770; although grown as a curiosity at Kew in 1772, it was not until 1819 that it was grown as a vegetable. It is widely available but not commonly grown, though the tender shoots and leaves can be eaten raw in salads or cooked as a vegetable.

PLANTING HELP   New Zealand spinach is usually grown as an annual. The seeds should be planted in late spring when there is no danger of frost, or they may be started indoors and planted out, at least 18in (45cm) apart. New Zealand spinach does best in deep sandy soil and will soon cover a considerable area. Once established, the plants are tolerant of drought, but if they are watered well in dry weather they will produce a better crop. Pinch out and eat the tips of the shoots when they are about 3in (8cm) long and they will then produce ample side shoots.

Ice Plant

A creeping annual or overwintering biennial, Ice Plant, *Mesembryanthemum cristallinum* is native to the SW Cape area of South Africa. It also grows wild in the Mediterranean region and Arabia, usually near the coast on dunes and in salt marshes and is naturalized in California. The common name refers to the fact that the surfaces of the leaves are covered in crystal-like cells which give them an appearance similar to hoar-frost. It has thick, fleshy leaves and stems and is grown as a substitute for spinach in hot climates but its juicy leaves with a touch of saltiness about them make an excellent addition to salads.

PLANTING HELP   In warm, frost-free climates, Ice Plant seeds should be sown in late summer, preferably in fertile soil, so that the young leaves can be harvested throughout the winter and spring. In cold climates the seeds should be sown indoors in late spring and transplanted when the danger of frost is over. They can then be harvested throughout summer and into early autumn when they often have a growth spurt with the onset of cooler weather. Slugs sometimes attack Ice Plants in wet condtions.

'Rhubarb Chard' in the Ballymaloe Cookery School Garden near Cork in Southern Ireland

Beet & Chard

Beet has been developed into a wide range of vegetables nearly as diverse as those provided by the cabbage. Wild Beet, Chard and 'Perpetual Spinach Beet' provide edible leaves or leaf stalks, while swollen-rooted beets produce beetroot, the red root commonly eaten as either a salad or hot vegetable, and Mangolds, which are used as winter feed for stock. Sugar Beet is a very widely grown source of sugar, second only to sugar cane. Napoleon encouraged its cultivation in the Napoleonic Wars when Britain cut off the West Indian supplies of sugar to France. Beets and chards have been grown for centuries in Europe and in Asia; Aristotle mentions red chards in his writings; and the Chinese are as keen on growing them in the 20th century as they were in the 7th century.

PLANTING HELP   Beets and chards are among the easiest and most productive vegetables to grow, providing they have plenty of water and nitrogen. They flourish in rich, moist soil with plenty of manure. Either sow the seed indoors in early spring and put the young plants out a month later or plant the seeds *in situ* and thin to 1ft (30cm) apart. In dry, well-drained soil, place the young plants in a shallow trench to make watering more efficient. As all beets respond well to salt, work 1oz per square yard (30 gms per square m) plus some potash into the soil a week before planting. Sometimes a second crop can be sown in August to harvest the following summer. To harvest, pull or cut off single leaves at ground level and use either in salads or cooked as a vegetable.

'Conrad'   A beet with glossy green leaves.

'Lucullus'   An improved variety of Seakale beet which has broad, light green, crinkly leaves and wide midribs.

'Perpetual Spinach Beet'   A tough variety with wide leaf blades and narrow ribs, which makes an excellent spinach substitute in summer.

'Rhubarb Chard'

BEET & CHARD

Wild Beet or Sea Beet

'Perpetual Spinach Beet'

'Lucullus'

'Conrad'

'Rhubarb Chard' This has crimson stalks and green leaves which look very dramatic and are excellent grown in a potager or in pots. Both stems and leaves are rich in vitamins and can be eaten, but it is generally a good idea to separate the leaves from the stems before cooking.

Wild Beet or Sea Beet *Beta vulgaris* subsp. *maritima* A common seaside plant, generally perennial, found in S and W Europe, North Africa and Asia, generally on shingle beaches just above the high tide mark. It has fleshy leaf blades which, together with the stems, are usually green although they sometimes show traces of the red colour characteristic of the garden beetroot. The young leaves of Sea Beet make an excellent substitute for spinach.

Common Sorrel in flower with wild Thrift in the background

Sorrel

Sorrel is a very hardy perennial plant with several varieties. It has been used for centuries for medicinal and culinary purposes and was a very popular pot herb and salad plant in medieval times. Its leaves have a sharp acid, tangy taste. They can be used sparingly in salads or made into a soup or puréed as a sauce for fish, particularly oily fish as the acidity of the sauce counteracts the richness of the fish. The leaves can be used to make a tea reputed to be effective as a diuretic or laxative. High in oxalic acid, sorrel should not be eaten continuously as this can lead to the formation of small stones of calcium oxalate.

PLANTING HELP   Sorrel will grow in most soils but does best in rich soil in cool, moist conditions in a sheltered or lightly shaded spot. It can be cultivated either by root division if you find some in the wild or grown from seed. Sow seeds in spring or autumn either *in situ* or in seed boxes for transplanting and then thinning out to about 10in (25cm) apart. When they are big enough, pick the outer leaves and leave the inner core of leaves to produce more. Cut off the seed heads to conserve the plant's energy. Replace old plants after three or four years before they become too woody.

Common Sorrel, Garden Sorrel *Rumex acetosa* An erect perennial native to Europe, temperate Asia, North America and Greenland, where it grows wild in grassland, meadows and open woods. Most of the broad arrow-shaped leaves come from the base of the plant which puts up a simple flowering stem with a few leaves.

Large-leaved Sorrel   The cultivated form of the wild species has much larger, thinner leaves with a milder and less acidic flavour.

French Sorrel, Buckler-leaved Sorrel *Rumex scutatus*   A perennial native to C and S Europe, W Asia and North Africa where it grows on old walls, in mountain pastures and on screes. It is distinguished from Common Sorrel by its finer, more lemony flavour, its smaller size and succulent shield-shaped leaves. It thrives in drier and better-drained soil than Common Sorrel and this, together with its less bitter flavour, probably accounts for its great popularity in France.

Herb Patience *Rumex patientia*   A hardy perennial native to E Europe, Turkey, N Asia and North Africa where it grows on waste land and open grassland. It grows to 7ft (2m) tall with long leaves to 1ft (30cm). Commonly cultivated in the past, seed is still available and the advantage of this variety is that it is less bitter than the others and comes into growth earlier in the year (*not illustrated*).

SORREL

Wild Sorrel

French Sorrel

Large-leaved Sorrel

Different species of sorrel

cooked and served cold with vinaigrette as is the custom in Italy. As the iron for which spinach is valued (especially by pregnant women and those with anæmia) is soluble, the water that cooking spinach produces should not be thrown away but evaporated with butter and stirred back into the cooked leaves. Eating tomatoes or oranges in the same meal as spinach is highly recommended as it will greatly increase the absorption of iron.

PLANTING HELP   Spinach grows best in rich moist soil with a high nitrogen content. Seed of hardier varieties is usually sown in late summer or early autumn and will stand through the winter if protected by frames or cloches. It can then be harvested until late spring. Tender varieties should be sown from early spring onwards for an early summer crop and further sowings can be made throughout the summer in cool areas. Seeds should be sown thinly and the plants spaced 6–10in (15–25cm) apart. Young plants must never be allowed to dry out and will benefit from waterings of high-nitrogen liquid fertilizer during growth; application of salt at the rate of 1oz per square yard (30 gms per square m) is especially beneficial in wet climates. The most serious threat to producing a good crop is bolting, caused by too little water in hot dry weather; pests and diseases are rarely a major problem.

'Sigmaleaf'

Spinach

A quick-growing annual, *Spinachia oleracea* probably originated in SW Asia or the Himalayas and was first cultivated by the Persians. It spread into Europe in the 11th century when it was introduced to Spain by the Arabs before it reached England in the 16th century. It is not certain from which wild species the cultivated form originated.

Spinach can be used in salads, soups, quiches, stir-fries or as a steamed or boiled vegetable. Young leaves are delicious raw, either as a salad on their own or mixed with other leaves; older leaves are better lightly cooked and served with butter, or

'King of Denmark'   A hardy dark green spinach variety with savoyed upright leaves. In good conditions in North America this spinach can mature in about 46 days.

'Longstanding Round'   A quick-maturing spinach of the round-seeded variety.

'Sigmaleaf'   A robust spinach variety that grows to 1ft (30cm) tall. It has leaves that are broadly arrow-shaped with a blistered surface and is suitable for spring or autumn sowing.

Spinach leaves

SPINACH

'Longstanding Round'

'King of Denmark'

Spinach growing in Thomas Jefferson's vegetable garden at Monticello in Virginia, USA

Ceylon Spinach & Malabar Spinach

These two fast-growing annuals are tropical climbers often grown as substitutes for spinach. They twine up any support and produce a plentiful supply of fleshy leaves that have a similar flavour but a slightly slimier texture than true spinach when cooked. As well as being grown for culinary purposes *Basella* also has medicinal and cosmetic properties: in China the roots are used to treat diarrhoea and the leaves act as a gentle laxative. The red fruits of var. *rubra* can be used as a food dye or rouge.

PLANTING HELP   Both these plants are easy to cultivate provided they have sufficient heat. Sow indoors in spring, so that there is enough heat for the seeds to germinate, around 68°F (20°C). Soak the seeds first to improve the chances of germination. After germination, a temperature of 60°F (16°C) is needed for good growth, so in N Europe these plants are best grown in a greenhouse. In warm North American conditions a crop is ready in about 70 days.

Ceylon Spinach *Basella rubra*   Probably native to S India but now widely grown in China and SE Asia, this plant has reddish leaves and deep red fruits formed by fleshy petals.

Malabar Spinach *Basella rubra* var. *alba*   Also probably native to southern India but now grown widely in China and SE Asia, this variety has green leaves (*not illustrated*).

Chickweed

An annual or overwintering herb, Chickweed *Stellaria media* is native to Europe and naturalized throughout most of the world. A very common weed, it is found growing along streams and roads and in fields, gardens and waste places. Although sometimes considered to be a troublesome and invasive weed, chickweed has been used as a medicinal and culinary plant since the Middle Ages. The whole plant can be eaten raw in salads, or cooked as a vegetable that is very similar to spinach, or used to make a delicious soup. In former times it was made into a poultice or an ointment to soothe wounds, ulcers and skin irritations.

PLANTING HELP   Chickweed is very easily found in the wild or will spread rapidly if introduced into bare ground in the garden.

Ceylon Spinach

Miner's Lettuce

An attractive annual, *Montia perfoliata* is native to W North America and naturalized in W Europe. Sometimes called Spring Beauty or Winter Purslane, it is found growing wild on rather dry sandy soils, along roadsides and on lower mountain slopes. The leaves have a mild fresh taste and make a cress-like addition to salads. They are particularly useful in spring as they provide young green leaves at a time when little else is available. The common name derives from the fact that it was eaten by miners during the American gold rush of the 1850s as a means of preventing scurvy when green vegetables were in short supply.

PLANTING HELP   Miner's Lettuce will grow on light sandy soils or in ordinary garden soil provided that it is not allowed to dry out or become waterlogged. The best position is in the shade of a deciduous tree, if possible. It is best grown from seed sown *in situ* in summer, to provide leaves the following spring. The plants will need to be covered with cloches over the winter to protect them, both from extreme cold and too much rain, neither of which they like.

Chickweed

Miner's Lettuce

Celery & Celeriac

Wild celery, which is native to Europe and Asia, is a strong-smelling biennial that can be found growing in damp places near the sea or in mud on the edges of tidal rivers and marshlands. In ancient times it was used medicinally in a variety of ways including as a stimulant, a diuretic and as a tonic for rheumatism. In the 17th century, the Italians began to develop the cultivated form of celery which we commonly use today. It was valued then, as it is now, as an important vegetable for the many vitamins and minerals it contains.

Celery is now eaten in three distinct forms: var. *dulce* is the commonest, consisting of the swollen leaf stems that are known as celery; var. *rapaceum* is the swollen rootstock that we call celeriac; and var. *secalinum* is the leafy celery which is very pungent and used as a herb for flavouring. This is similar to one grown in China where they cook the leaves and stems together in a green and unblanched state. A cut-leaved variety of this is now sold under the name 'Parcel'.

Celery can be eaten cooked or raw. It is a popular component of *crudités*, makes delicious soup, is added to stews and stir-fries and is an excellent accompaniment to cheese, counteracting its richness and aiding digestion.

Celery 'Golden Self-blanching' at Villandry

PLANTING HELP   Celery needs a rich moist soil to grow well and must have at least 5 gallons per square yard (18 litres per square metre) of water per week to thrive. Seedlings are best raised indoors in spring. Take care when planting out because damage at this stage can cause bolting.

Self-blanching celery is best grown in blocks instead of rows as a certain amount of blanching improves the stalks. Varieties that need blanching are usually grown in a single row in a trench 15in (40cm) wide and 12in (30cm) deep. When the plants are about 12in (30cm) tall, remove their outer leaves to reduce them to a single head and then about 3in (8cm) of soil should be added around the base of the plant. This should continue as the plant grows with plenty of watering during the whole process. Alternatively, blanching can be done by tying layers of newspaper or black polythene around the stems.

Celeriac is difficult to grow to the size of shop-bought specimens but the secret is to plant the seedlings in rich soil with added organic matter and give plenty of water throughout the summer and long growing season. Celeriac is hardier than celery and will last well through the winter if stored in sand or protected with straw and left in a cool place. Celery fly can be a serious pest for all celeries, attacking the leaves of young plants and slowing down their growth. Any damaged leaves should be removed and burnt. If the attack is serious the plants may need to be sprayed with nicotine and soft soap or a systemic insecticide.

'American Green', 'Greensnap'   A green-stemmed celery which does not need blanching.

'Giant Pink'   A pink- or red-stemmed celery with dark green leaves. The stems are paler if blanched and deeper coloured in cold weather.

'Tellus'

'Iram'

Celeriac specimens from Wisley

CELERY & CELERIAC

Wild celery

Leaves of Celeriac

'American Green'

'Ivory Tower'

'Giant Pink'

Celery specimens from NIAB, Cambridge England

'Golden Self-blanching'   A celery with pale golden yellow leaves and golden stems. It is best eaten young in late summer and is not very frost-hardy.

'Ivory Tower'   A pale-leaved celery with narrow petioles that is self-blanching and quick-maturing. It needs plenty of water to prevent it from becoming dry and stringy.

'Iram'   A medium-sized celeriac with globe-shaped roots and few side roots.

'Tellus'   A quick-growing celeriac with medium-sized, globe-shaped roots and brownish red leaf stems.

Celery being blanched with brown paper

Lettuce

All lettuces have been developed from the wild species *Lactuca serriola*, which can be found in clearings in woods, waste places and on rocky slopes from Asia to North Africa and N Europe. It is a winter annual, germinating in the autumn to form conspicuous rosettes of leaves which flower in late summer the following year. Another species *Lactuca virosa* is similar in appearance and has been used in the breeding of such varieties as 'Vanguard'. Other wild species are found in the mountains of Turkey, Iran and the S Caucasus, and the woods and plains of North America, including *Lactuca canadensis*, sometimes called wild opium, and *Lactuca indica*, a perennial with spear-shaped leaves native to China, and cultivated there and in Indonesia for use as a cooked vegetable and a salad.

Lettuces are thought to have first been cultivated by the Egyptians around 4500 BC, though possibly for the oil from the seeds rather than as a salad. The Romans probably introduced lettuce to Britain as a plant food, and by 1597 there were eight varieties listed in Gerard's *Herball*. Readers of Beatrix Potter's *Peter Rabbit* will know that lettuces are soporific – sleep inducing – a quality recognized since ancient times and is mentioned by the great Greek physician Hippocrates in the 5th century BC. The bitter white latex or milk found in lettuces has often been used as a substitute for opium or laudanum.

Intensive breeding of numerous varieties has escalated over the centuries in Europe and North America. Modern breeders have concentrated on developing resistance to disease and bolting, as well as extending the variety of shapes and colours. Lettuces in their various forms are the most important salad crops, and are now available all year round since the introduction of types that can be grown under glass in winter.

The heavy crisp Iceberg lettuces, so popular in America, were developed to survive transportation from the West Coast to markets on the East Coast. Looser, softer cabbage-like lettuces are more common in N Europe and Cos lettuces are much favoured in the eastern Mediterranean. Celtuce, a variety grown in China which has swollen, crisp, fleshy stalks, is sliced for use in stir-fries. While in the West lettuces are principally used raw in green salads, mixed salads and garnish, in China they are generally cooked as a vegetable and added to soups and stir-fries. They are cooked for a very few moments at great heat to preserve colour and texture. Lettuces are also used raw to wrap minced food in a similar manner to the way thin pancakes are used to wrap Peking Duck.

'Bubbles'

PLANTING HELP Lettuces need rich well-drained soil with plenty of compost dug in and continual watering during the growing season if they are to thrive. Premature drying out causes the lettuces to go to seed early before they have developed their full size. Seeds for early spring and autumn crops are best grown in boxes or soil blocks indoors and then planted out when they are at the four- or five-leaf stage. Seeds require cool conditions to germinate and may become dormant above 68F (20°C). Late spring and summer varieties can be planted *in situ* and then thinned: 6in (15cm) apart for small lettuces and up to 14in (35cm) apart for the larger Cos and Iceberg types.

As well as being prey to the normal slugs and snails, lettuces are particularly attractive to aphids and cutworms, the lettuce root aphid *Pemphigus*

Red lettuces at Dry Gulch Organic Farm, California

LETTUCE

bursarius being the worst. This aphid attacks in July, August and September by crowding round the taproot, causing it to weaken and collapse. You can either spray the aphids with insecticidal soap or derris or if the problem is acute, choose a variety like 'Debbie' which has been bred to be resistant to root aphid. Cutworms are best controlled by going out at night with a torch and picking them off the base of the plants or by killing the young caterpillars with a fierce watering in early June before they have had time to eat into the root of the lettuce.

'Bubbles' A compact plant with medium green blistered leaves and a fairly firm head like 'Little Gem' but with a sweeter flavour. Suitable for early crops.

'Debbie' A modern variety with a compact firm head up to 12in (30cm) across; suitable for growing in polytunnels or frames

'Debbie'

A variety of lettuces at Joy Larkcom's garden in Suffolk, England

33

'Goya'

'Merveille de Quatre Saisons'

'Crispino'

'Webb's Wonderful'

'Cindy'   A large pale green butterhead with heads about 12in (30cm) across. It is not bitter and the head is held well above the soil; maturing in about 57 days in North America.

'Continuity' 'Brune Continuité', 'Bronze Beauty', 'Crisp as Ice', 'Hartford Bronzehead' A crisp butterhead with a small, tight, sweet heart good for growing in summer and tolerant of heat. The wavy leaves are often reddish; it matures in 65–70 days in North America.

'Webb's Wonderful', 'New York'   The original 'Webb's Wonderful' was reputedly introduced into North America in 1890 as a development of an old variety dating back to the mid-19th century. Further development resulted in the 'Imperial', 'Great Lakes' and 'New York' groups of varieties. Nowadays the term 'Webb's' is used as a generic name for a crisphead lettuce. **'Crispino'** is a small to medium crisphead with frilled leaves. Best in midsummer.

'Goya'   A new very red loose-leaf Dutch variety which is semi-Cos with no heart.

'Merveille de Quatre Saisons', 'Besson Rouge', 'Red Besson'   An old butterhead variety grown in the 19th century; it has dark reddish brown leaves and is popular in France and South America.

LETTUCE

'Cindy' a butterhead type

A cos lettuce *(left)* and 'Continuity' (*right*)

'Red Salad Bowl'

'Red Cos'

'Winter Density' (*left*) and 'Red Cos'

LETTUCE

'Salad Bowl' and 'Red Sails' (*right*)

'Green Ice'

'Saladisi' at Ryton Organic Garden

'Green Ice' A Batavian semi-Cos leaf lettuce with dark green leaves and crisped edges. It matures within 45 days in North America and has a good shelf-life and a long cutting season, as well as being resistant to powdery mildew.

'Saladisi', 'Misticanza', 'Mesclun', A mixture of salads which are sown thickly and eaten young, the leaves being cut and the plants encouraged to resprout. It may contain all or most of the following: lettuce, endive, chicory, dandelion, chervil, rocket, mustard and Buck's Horn Plaintain.

'Red Salad Bowl', 'Stuuwelpeter Gelber Krauser' A red-pigmented loose-leaf lettuce developed from Oak Leaf. Slow to bolt.

'Red Cos', 'Rouge d'Hiver', 'Red Winter', 'Red Roman' An old Cos or Romaine type lettuce with red leaves which is tolerant of heat and wet, and is fast growing; is best grown quickly with plenty of water.

'Red Sails' A Batavian loose-leaf lettuce with crinkled deep bronze red leaves. It is slow to bolt and matures in 45 days in North America.

'Salad Bowl' This is similar to Oak Leaf but takes as much as a month longer to bolt.

'Winter Density' A semi-Cos type of lettuce but larger, darker and slower to mature. The heart has a rounded top and a well-blanched centre; it is slow to bolt and is cold-resistant.

Endives with pots for blanching

Chicory & Endive

These two salad vegetables are very closely related to one another; the main differences being that endive is an annual plant whereas chicory is a perennial, and endive leaves are always hairless while chicory leaves are frequently hairy. Chicory is native to Europe and W Asia and is naturalized in North America where its beautiful blue flowers are a common sight on roadsides. The origin of endive is uncertain. Some believe it originated in N China, others think that it is a hybrid between chicory and a wild annual species native to Turkey and western Syria.

Both chicory and endive have a long history of medicinal and culinary use. There is evidence that endive was grown by the ancient Egyptians and from thence it became one of the bitter herbs used at Passover. The classical writers Horace, Pliny and Aristophanes, mention both in their writings, referring to their use as salad and cooked vegetables. Chicory was believed to be good for sore eyes and as a digestive, and the leaves were made into a poultice for swellings and inflammations. However, chicory is most well known as an adulterant to coffee, the roasted ground roots giving it a dark colour and bitterish taste that is particularly popular on the Continent.

Chicory and endive are also commonly grown as vegetable and salad plants, and the numerous varieties that have long been popular in France and Italy (where it is called *radicchio*) are now becoming more widely available elsewhere. Chicory and endive are excellent salad plants to grow because they are hardy, disease-resistant and are grown from autumn to spring when there is not a great deal of other salad available. Their distinctive, bitter taste makes a delicious addition to mixed salads, or they can be made into a salad on their own with sliced oranges, the sweetness of the orange contrasting with the bitterness of the chicory. It is also good with walnuts and stilton. Alternatively, chicory is delicious baked, as cooking reduces the bitter taste.

PLANTING HELP   Chicories are grown in two distinct ways: either they are grown to produce a large root which is then forced to provide chicons; or they are grown like lettuce to produce leafy salad plants. To produce chicons plant seeds of 'Witloof' chicory in late spring or early summer in deep soil (chalky or sandy) in open ground. Water and fertilize the plants well so that they build up a strong root system and thin to 6in (15cm) apart. In late autumn, when the temperatures are near freezing, dig the plants up a few at a time and force them indoors. Trim the roots, which should be at least 1½in (4cm) in diameter, and cut back the foliage to within ¾in (2cm) of the top of the root, then plant the roots in moist peat, in a large plastic pot (about 3–5 per pot), keeping them warm and totally dark as any light getting through to the leaves causes them to become bitter. Forced indoors the chicons are usually produced in three weeks. If you wish to blanch them more slowly outdoors you can trim back the leaves and then cover the plants with 8in (20cm) of peat or sand. They should be picked before reaching the light in early spring. This slower method produces sweeter, more flavourful chicons. Other varieties of chicory, including red-leaved types, can also be blanched in this manner.

'Sugarloaf' chicories and endive are grown in a similar way to lettuce. Seed can either be sown in early spring for a summer crop or after midsummer for an autumn crop and the plants take two to three months to mature. In cold climates the heads need to be protected from frost either by being cut and stored in a cool place or by being protected in the ground under a cloche. 'Sugarloaf' chicories need no blanching and the red-leaved varieties can either be cut direct from the garden or forced like 'Witloof'. Endives often

Endive 'Coquette'

CHICORY & ENDIVE

'Snowflake'

'Alouette'
(*text page 40*)

'Coquette'

Specimens from Sellindge, Kent

need blanching. The leaves can either be tied up so that the hearts are kept dark or the whole plant can be covered with a large plastic or clay pot. In mild climates the plants can be sown in autumn and overwintered for harvesting in early spring.

'Coquette' A variety of curled endive which can be sown in late summer for harvesting throughout the winter.

'Green Curled', 'Moss Curled', 'Chicorée Frisée' A variety of endive with finely cut and crisped leaves. The leaves are often tied or the plant covered with a dark pot to blanch the centre and make it less bitter.

'Snowflake', 'Winter Fare' An easily grown variety of the Sugarloaf type with very thin leaves. It is best planted in midsummer in rich moist soil and harvested in autumn and winter

'Sugarloaf', 'Pan di Zucchero', 'Pain de Sucre' Large and rather cabbage-like plants with hearts somewhat self-blanching and only slightly bitter. This is best sown in midsummer and used in autumn or through the winter if protected by frames or cloches.

Chicory 'Sugarloaf'

Endive 'Green Curled'

39

CHICORY & RADICCHIO

'Witloof', 'Brussel Witloof', 'Belgian Chicory' This chicory is nearest to the wild form. The plants have rather upright dark green lobed leaves and are used as a winter vegetable when blanched. A well-grown root should be short and thick to produce the fattest chicons.

'Alouette' A variety of radicchio with a good red heart and white ribs; has a good flavour and a crisp texture. Sow in early summer for harvest in autumn and winter (*illustration page 39*).

'Red Treviso', 'Rosso di Treviso' A red-leaved radicchio with large, tight, round hearts and leaves with rather narrow white midribs and veins. Good for winter salads or lightly cooked.

'Red Treviso' forced in the dark

'Variegata di Chioggia' From Chioggia in Italy, this decorative radicchio has a round head and is variegated in the winter.

Flowers of chicory with mint

Spring leaves of radicchio 'Red Treviso'

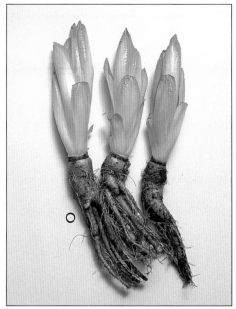

Forced chicons of 'Witloof'

Radicchio 'Variegata di Chioggia'

PLANTING HELP   Asparagus is very easy to grow provided it is planted in a sheltered place, in full sun and well-drained soil. Sow seed in early spring, either indoors or in a seed bed outdoors, in very sandy, well-drained soil, set out in a shallow trench on a slight ridge. On heavy, cold or wet soils it is worth making a raised bed. The young plants should be grown on carefully for the first year and the first cutting should be possible when the plants are three years old, but this should be for no more than six weeks. Established beds are generally cut for eight weeks. When the bed is established it should be top dressed with fertilizer in early spring and mulched in winter with old manure. Salt is traditionally applied in May to September which discourages most weeds and slugs and, according to some, increases the yield.

'Lucullus'   An all-male variety which produces good spears.

Asparagus spears

Asparagus

Asparagus officinalis comes from a large genus of about 300 species that are found throughout Asia and Africa and while most are tough climbers, their fleshy, young stems are edible. Asparagus is found wild all over Europe, Africa and Asia east to Iran, growing in sandy places, dry meadows, on limestone cliffs and volcanic hillsides. Asparagus was first mentioned by the Greeks as a vegetable but it may only have been collected from the wild. However, the Romans had elaborate methods for producing huge, blanched stems and by the 16th century it was such a profitable crop that in Venice it displaced the growing of flax and corn.

Asparagus 'Lucullus'

SPRING ONIONS & WELSH ONIONS

'Ishiko Straight Leaf'

'White Flash'

'Savel'

'White Lisbon'

'Hikari Bunching'

'Yoshima'

'Guardsman'

'White Knight'

'Winter White Bunching'

'Winter Over'

Welsh onion specimens from NIAB, Cambridge, England

Onions

Small onions or alliums of various kinds have been used for centuries in cooking and medicine. They are also an important ingredient in soups, stews, meat, fish and vegetable dishes and in sauces and salads. All onions are reputed to increase longevity and general health by aiding digestion. High in vitamin C and other vitamins and minerals, they were, in the past, eaten to ward off scurvy and keep infectious diseases at bay. They are also reputed to aid memory, concentration and creative thought. The flavour is much stronger if eaten raw but they do not always agree with those people who suffer from wind.

Spring Onions

These smaller specimens of the common onion *Allium cepa*, have a long neck and small bulb, and are sometimes called green or bunching onions or scallions. Used raw in salads or finely chopped in soups, they are a great favourite in Chinese cooking in which both the bulbs and stalks are used.

PLANTING HELP   Spring onion seeds should be sown in summer in the north and autumn in the south to give crops the following spring; if they are sown in spring they will give summer crops. There should be about 30 plants in a 1ft (30cm) square, and as they grow quickly, plenty of water will be needed in dry weather.

Welsh Onions

This onion *Allium fistulosum* forms large perennial clumps and is like very large coarse chives. It has hollow evergreen leaves and almost no bulb at the base. Sometimes called Japanese bunching onions or Chinese small onions, they are used by both cultures as a flavouring in stir-fried vegetables; in winter they can be used raw as a substitute for chives. Welsh onion has been grown in China since prehistoric times but it is unclear how it became associated with Wales. It is thought that the name may be derived from the German word *welsche* which means 'foreign'.

PLANTING HELP   Welsh onions are grown in the same way as spring onions. The soil should be well drained but moist in the growing season and, although modern varieties are self-blanching, the stem portion can be increased by earthing up the plants with 8in (20cm) of soil.

'Guardsman'   A hybrid between *A. cepa* and *A. fistulosum* which stands well without becoming strong flavoured or bulbing.

Flowering Welsh onion

'Hikari Bunching'   A cultivar of *A. fistulosum* with slight bulbing and good botrytis resistance.

'Ishiko Straight Leaf'   A cultivar of *A. fistulosum* with slight bulbing and bluish leaves.

'Savel'   A cultivar of *A. fistulosum* with no bulbing and good botrytis resistance.

'White Flash'   A hybrid between *A. cepa* and *A. fistulosum* with slight bulbing; good for over-wintering.

'White Knight'   A cultivar of *A. cepa* which is more bulbous than most with dark green leaves.

'White Lisbon'   A cultivar of *A. cepa* with some bulbing; quite hardy.

'Winter Over', 'White Lisbon Winter Hardy' A cultivar of *A. cepa*, it is the hardiest of all the varieties. It is rather bulbous with dark green leaves and is susceptible to botrytis.

'Winter White Bunching'   A cultivar of *A. cepa* which is slightly more bulbous than average and moderately hardy.

'Yoshima'   A cultivar of *A. fistulosum* that is more bulbous than most.

43

Garden chives

Chives

A perennial plant forming tufts of narrow bulbs, *Allium schoenoprasum* is found wild in the mountains of Europe, from England to Siberia, and in Japan. Chives usually grow in damp meadows, by streams and lake shores. The slender hollow leaves of chives are generally used as a flavouring or garnish for salads, cold potatoes and egg dishes and can be used raw or dried.

PLANTING HELP   Chives can be grown either from seed or by dividing old clumps in spring or autumn. They will do best in a cool place in moist well-drained soil. Plant seeds in a soil block, preferably indoors, and then transplant the seedlings outside as a group together otherwise they will easily get lost. Divide old clumps every three years by pulling up the whole clump and separating three or four small plants from the outer edge of the clump and replanting them apart from the other clumps. Make sure to keep watering them in hot weather.

Chinese Chives

A perennial plant, *Allium tuberosum* forms dense clumps and has tall flowering stems and umbels of white flowers. Chinese chives are thought to be native to China, the eastern Himalayas and possibly also Japan. In China they are used as a vegetable rather than as a flavouring and the leaves are blanched so that they look like pale straw. To do this the Chinese prop large tiles along the rows and seal the gaps or suspend mats on either side of the plants. The leaves are very pleasantly flavoured – a cross between garlic and chives – and they, together with the flower heads and stalks, can be used in salads

PLANTING HELP   Chinese chives may be raised from seed or by dividing established clumps. They tolerate a variety of soils and conditions but they prefer a good, rich, moist, well-drained soil. Plant seeds in spring or autumn and only cut the leaves when they have reached at least 6in (15cm) high. Do not allow the plants to flower and use sparingly until the second year when you have established a good clump. They can also be grown effectively in a flower pot.

Garlic

Garlic *Allium sativum,* is a bulbous perennial that has been grown since 3200 BC in Egypt, is not known in the wild except as an escape. Garlic is thought to have been derived from *Allium longicuspis*, a native of central Asia. The distinctive

Chinese chives

GARLIC & CHINESE CHIVES

Garlic harvest, Green Gulch Farm, California

and highly flavoured bulbs of the garlic plant have been cultivated for centuries for both medicinal and culinary uses. Garlic was thought to impart strength and it was an essential ingredient in the diet of the labourers building the pyramids. It is also recognized as having numerous antibiotic, antiseptic and antibacterial properties and modern research has confirmed that it is beneficial at keeping amoebic dysentery at bay and reducing blood cholesterol. It is a basic ingredient of nearly all Chinese cooking and of much of the cooking of S and E Europe as well. It is used to flavour soups, stews, sauces, salads, stir-fries, meat, fish and vegetables either cooked or raw.

PLANTING HELP   Garlic is now propagated vegetatively and does not set fertile seed. To grow garlic, set some single cloves firmly in the ground, in sandy soil in a warm position, in spring if in a climate with a cold winter, in autumn if in a Mediterranean climate. These often make solid bulbs or 'rounds' in the first year, but if kept over winter and planted again the next spring they will form a large multi-cloved bulb. These should be harvested in late July and dried in the sun before storing for use over the winter.

Field of garlic near Ili in Sinjiang, Central Asia

Garlic cloves

Blanched Chinese chives on sale in China

45

'Tokyo Cross'

'Purple Top
Milan'

'Purple Top
White Globe'

Turnip varieties

Turnip

Turnips, like oil-seed turnip rape and many kinds of Chinese cabbage, were developed from *Brassica rapa,* which is divided into several subspecies including subspecies *sylvestris* and *rapa.* Subspecies *sylvestris* is the wild type, found commonly all over Europe, North America and much of Asia, growing as a weed by streams or on open ground. Subspecies *rapa* is the cultivated turnip. The edible fleshy taproot is usually round in most European varieties, but the Chinese and Japanese varieties are often long, narrow and carrot-shaped. Present-day varieties are grown with either white or yellow flesh and yellow, white, green or purple-topped skins. Turnip roots can either be eaten cooked in stews and soups, as a separate vegetable, or they can be grated and eaten raw in salads. The young seedling leaves can also be added to salads and the larger leaves are used for spring greens in Europe.

Kohlrabi 'White Vienna'

Kohlrabi in China

Kohlrabi

Kohlrabi, which originated in northern Europe in the 15th century, is an oddly shaped form of cabbage, *Brassica oleracea*, with a very short stem that swells into a large edible, corm-like ball. These are best eaten when young (up to the size of a tennis ball) and although they are generally cooked, the nutty sweet flavour is excellent chopped, grated or sliced raw in salads. Kohlrabi is a highly nutritious vegetable, rich in protein, calcium and vitamin C, and is found in two skin colours, white or pale green and purple; the white varieties being the sweetest, the purple varieties the hardiest. It is fast growing and more tolerant of drought than most brassicas and it matures in 40–70 days.

PLANTING HELP   Kohlrabi needs fertile, light, moist soils and seed can be sown *in situ* from very early spring (in warm gardens) to early autumn. Plants should be about 10in (25cm) apart and kept well watered if they are to grow steadily. Cabbage root fly, and on acid soil, clubroot, are the pests and diseases to watch out for.

Kohlrabi 'White Vienna'   This traditional cultivar with pale green skin is still commonly grown.

Kohlrabi 'Purple Vienna'   Another traditional cultivar with purple skin that remains popular.

PLANTING HELP   Turnips are easy to grow and very hardy, and will be ready about 70 days after sowing provided they are kept well watered when young. For an early summer crop, sow under cover in late winter or *in situ* in early spring, and harvest small for delicious sweet turnips. For overwintering sow in mid- to late summer, thinning out to about 6in (15cm) and make sure they have plenty of water if the weather is dry, since drying out and attacks by cabbage root fly are the commonest causes of failure.

'Purple Top Milan'   This early maturing variety has flattish white roots with purple markings and is good for overwintering.

'Purple Top White Globe'   This old variety with round or slightly flattened roots is reddish purple above ground and white below. It is now considered the same as 'Veitch's Red Globe'.

'Tokyo Cross'   Raised in Japan, this quick-maturing and heat-tolerant variety has round white roots and is suitable for sowing in midsummer for an autumn crop.

Kohlrabi 'Purple Vienna'

47

'Tsukushi Spring Cross' (*left*) and 'Minowasi Summer No. 2 '

'April Cross'

Radish

Radishes have been cultivated since Egyptian times when they were included in the rations given to the workers on the Great Pyramid. Although the origin of the cultivated radish is not known, it was presumably developed from the wild species which is commonly found on sandy wasteland, both by the sea and inland across much of Europe. By 500 BC radish was cultivated in China and by AD 700 it was grown in Japan. In both countries it is an important root vegetable eaten raw, cooked and preserved or often carved into an elaborate garnish. Although in Europe it is only a minor salad plant, radish is becoming more widely known with the increasing interest in Oriental cuisine.

Modern cultivated radishes are usually divided into four groups: White or Red radishes, Black radishes, Mougri radish (grown for its long, edible seed pods), and Oil-seed radish. White or Red radishes are grown in Europe as quick-maturing

Radishes, similar to the variety 'China Rose' in the market in Ili, Chinese Central Asia

RADISH

salad plants eaten young and raw. Black radishes are the most ancient group and were popular in the 17th century as they lasted through the winter. Nowadays both round and long varieties with rather rough black or dark brown skins are available from Spain and Italy. Most Chinese and Japanese varieties are long and white and slow to mature, making them a useful winter vegetable for slicing and cooking in soups. Radish leaves and seedlings can also be cooked or added to salads.

PLANTING HELP
Small salad radishes are very quick and easy to grow. They need an open position and a light fine soil with adequate moisture to grow rapidly. Seed can be sown throughout the summer at one- or two-week intervals, aiming to get the seeds about 1in (2.5cm) apart. The quickest varieties can mature in twenty days. Black radishes should be sown in midsummer and thinned to 6in (15cm) apart. Care must be taken with watering as too little water will cause the roots to crack when it rains, and too much will make them produce leaf growth at the expense of the roots. Oriental radishes are a bit harder to grow and different varieties are adapted for sowing at different seasons. Most are best sown after midsummer and will be ready in autumn, winter and the following spring. They need at least 55 days to mature.

'Prinz Rotin'

'Pfitzer's Maindreieek'

'April Cross' An easily grown Oriental variety that will stand over winter from a summer sowing.

'Black Spanish Long' An old variety from the 19th century, which is suitable for eating raw and cooked like a Japanese radish.

'Black Spanish Round' An old variety with white flesh sown in midsummer for winter eating.

'Minowasi Summer No. 2' Japanese radish with long tapering roots. Sow in late spring or summer to harvest in autumn.

'Pfitzer's Maindreieek' A winter radish with brown skin and white flesh.

'Prinz Rotin', 'Red Prince' A globe variety that takes 25 days to mature and stands well.

'Tsukushi Spring Cross' A Japanese radish to sow in spring or early summer and harvest in summer and early autumn.

'Black Spanish Long' (*left*) 'Black Spanish Round'

'Regala'

Beetroot

Beetroot is one of the many diverse vegetables in the *Beta vulgaris* group which ranges from Chard to Sugar Beet to Perpetual Spinach *(pages 22–23)*. Beet has been cultivated for centuries, and red beetroots were developed by the Romans and continued to be called 'Roman beet' in the Middle Ages. Beetroots, usually called 'globe' beets, are red, round and swollen-rooted, and there are a large number of very similar cultivars. Some are semi-globe in shape with more tapering roots, others are long and cylindrical, suitable for slicing. Different colours are rare but there is a golden variety, a white variety and one with concentric rings of pink and white; all these colours have a similar flavour and look very pretty in salads. Beetroot can either be cooked and eaten hot or cold, or it can be grated and eaten raw. Young beetroot leaves can be used raw in salads or lightly cooked as a vegetable.

'Monogram'

'Red Ace'

'Detroit Lora'

'Detroit Little Ball'

'Cylindra'

'Mammoth Long'

Beetroot specimens from the Royal Horticultural Society's garden at Wisley

BEETROOT

'Albinia Verecunda' (*left*) and 'Burpee's Golden' (*right*). Specimens from Sellindge, Kent

PLANTING HELP   Beetroot needs an open position and light well-drained soil which has not been freshly manured. Seed should be sown in early spring and the plants thinned to about 6in (15cm) apart. The quickest varieties are ready in about two months. Later sowings in early summer can mature in 45 days, though at this season the larger, longer-maturing varieties and the cylindrical ones can be planted to last the winter. Beetroot suffers from few pests or diseases, though leaf spots may affect the leaves; this can be prevented by an application of potash before sowing.

'Albinia Verecunda'   An old variety with rounded roots and a very sweet flavour.

'Burpee's Golden'   Golden yellow, round roots and similar in flavour to the red varieties.

'Cylindra'   This has long cylindrical, dark red roots.

'Detroit Little Ball'   A fast-growing variety for a quick crop and resistant to bolting. Its flesh has distinct pale rings and the leaves are green with red stems.

'Detroit Lora'   This variety matures early and has a high yield which can be cropped when small.

'Mammoth Long'   A red long-rooted variety.

'Monogram'   A monogerm (with one seed per fruit, unlike most varieties which have several seeds in one fruit and therefore need thinning) variety with roots like a flattened sphere. Resistant to bolting.

'Red Ace'   Round red roots with very tender flesh. Resistant to bolting.

'Regala'   This variety has a purplish red round root with distinct zones and small green leaves. Resistant to bolting.

'J. O. Caropak'

'Early Horn'

Carrots planted next to onions

Carrots

The carrot is a member of the family *Umbelliferae* which contains parsnips, celery and parsley, as well as hemlock and other equally poisonous parsley-like plants. Wild carrot, which usually has white roots, is found throughout Europe and Asia, and in North America it has escaped from cultivation and become a pernicious weed in some areas. Cultivated carrots were certainly grown by the Romans, and it is thought that orange carrots were developed from red anthocyanin-containing carrots which can still be found wild in Afghanistan. Yellow carrots were first recorded in Turkey in the 10th century and both yellow and purple ones were popular throughout Europe until the 17th century when the orange carrot was developed in Holland.

Carrots are biennial. In the first year they produce the edible, fleshy, orange taproot and in the second year they produce flowers. The roots contain significant amounts of sugar and carotene, an orange pigment which is converted by the intestines into vitamin A, a deficiency of which can result in blindness in children. Carrots can be eaten raw or cooked: those known as 'earlies' are generally used raw or grated in salads, while those called 'maincrop' are mainly cultivated for use as a cooked vegetable.

PLANTING HELP   Carrots thrive in sandy soil that is chalky or well limed and prepared so that it is very loose and easily crumbled. Seed should be sown about ¾in (2cm) deep, aiming to produce about 20 plants per 1ft (30cm) square for medium-sized carrots, more for very small carrots and about 10 plants in the same area for large carrots. In the garden, seed is usually sown more ·

CARROTS

Netting used as protection against carrot root fly; the barrier is 2½ft (75cm) high

thickly than this, as the young carrots which are thinned out can be eaten. After they have been thinned, the soil should be drawn up along the row so that carrot root flies do not find an easy route to the remaining crop. This is the commonest and worst pest of carrots and is very hard to control.

Early sowings should be made in spring to in order to avoid the early crop of flies, and later sowings in summer have a good chance of avoiding attack. Placing barriers 2–3ft (60–90cm) high around the rows can help because the fly travels near the ground and is easily diverted.

Alternatively, planting sage or onions in among the carrots can help divert the carrot root fly from the smell of the carrots' foliage to which it is strongly attracted.

'Early Horn' An early-maturing variety, suitable for sowing under glass in winter for harvesting in late spring or early summer. Partially resistant to carrot root fly.

'J. O. Caropak' An Imperator-type with good resistance to bolting.

CARROTS

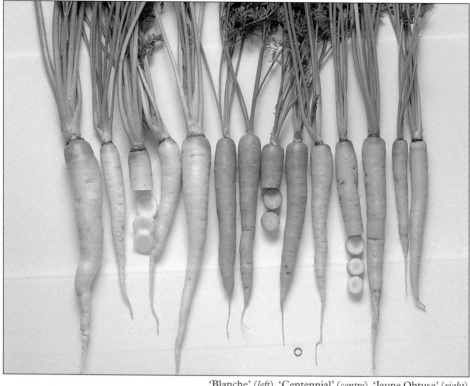

'Blanche' (*left*), 'Centennial' (*centre*), 'Jaune Obtuse' (*right*)

'Jaune Obtuse'

'Blanche'
An old Belgian white-rooted variety.

'Centennial'
An Imperator variety, inclined to bolt in Britain.

'Jaune Obtuse'
An old yellow-rooted variety, partially resistant to carrot root fly.

'Redca' A coreless carrot with good juice content. Suitable for pulling young at 6in (15cm) long, after about 70 days in North America.

'Redca'

'Salad Red'

Potatoes

The potato is the fourth most important food crop in the world after wheat, maize and rice. It grows well in all temperate climates and in many parts of the tropics, especially in the mountains or when grown in the cool season. The potato is a member of the *Solanaceae* family which includes the tomato, sweet and hot peppers, tobacco, deadly nightshade and other very poisonous plants. Although the edible potato tubers contain vitamins, protein and large amounts of starch, the fruit, sprouts and leaves are highly poisonous as they contain the alkaloid solanine as do any parts of the tubers that have turned green after exposure to light. Therefore they must never be eaten raw. Remains of potatoes, dating from 4000 BC were found in South America, but the first reports of potatoes in Europe date from the mid-16th century. By the 18th century the potato had become an important staple in the British Isles and during the following century breeders developed a range of interesting cultivars, many of which became the seed parents of modern varieties.

PLANTING HELP   Potatoes are the most easily grown of all vegetables, provided they have enough water and are protected from frost. Buy healthy seed potatoes from a reliable source, avoiding those that have pale sprouts. Plant the tubers in spring, about a month before the last frost, preferably in sandy soil with a high humus content, although they will tolerate chalky soil as well. As potatoes need ample nitrogen, it is beneficial to manure the ground the previous autumn with farmyard manure or garden compost, both of which will also help to retain moisture. On ordinary soils plant the tubers into a drill about 4in (10cm) deep and 15in (38cm) apart. Earth up the emerging shoots one

'Pink Fir Apple'

to three times in the growing season to prevent tubers from becoming green on exposure to light. Give the potatoes plenty of water while in full growth and extra water when the tubers are ⅓in (1cm) across will improve the size of the early potatoes
.
'Pink Fir Apple'   A salad variety with yellow waxy flesh and strong flavour.

'Salad Blue'   A striking purple-fleshed variety that looks and tastes excellent in a salad.

'Salad Red'   An old red-skinned variety.

'Salad Blue'

55

Mustard and cress

Sprouting Seeds

Sprouted seeds not only make a delicious addition to salads but are also very nutritious, sometimes having as much as twice the vitamin and mineral content of the mature leaves. Seeds may be sprouted in a jar in any warm dark place, although the easiest way is probably to follow the instructions given with the special sprouting trays which are now commonly available.

PLANTING HELP Seedlings can be grown outside or indoors. If grown outside they can be sown on areas awaiting other crops or between crops such as brassicas. They grow very quickly and can be cut as early as two weeks after sowing. Later in the year, seedlings can be planted under cover in greenhouses and frames that may

Bisai or Japanese radish

Mung beans

Manna

Fenugreek

Puy lentils (*left*) and Large
Green lentils

Adzuki beans

SPROUTING SEEDS

otherwise be empty. Alternatively, they can be grown indoors in a shallow seedtray or on blotting paper. Seedlings need to be kept moist and warm and can be cut as soon as they are an edible size, leaving at least 1in (2.5cm) in the ground. Keep cutting the seedlings regularly otherwise they will outgrow the seedling size, although many of them can still be eaten when the leaves are bigger.

Adzuki Beans *Vigna angularis* Best eaten after five days; if left until the leaves appear, they are usually too tall and stringy.

Alfalfa or **Lucerne** *Medicágo sativa* Nutritious, sweet-tasting sprouts that take from four to six days to grow.

Bisai or **Japanese Radish** *Raphanus sativus* These have a hot radishy flavour and are delicious in salads. They take six days to grow.

Curled Cress *Lepidium sativum* Most commonly grown cress, it takes about seven days to sprout. Also known as cress or common cress.

Mustard *Sinapis alba* This grows faster than Curled Cress so start Mustard about three days earlier if growing the two to eat at the same time.

Fenugreek *Trigonella foenum-graecum* Sprouts that have a mild curry flavour, delicious added to salads or served with curries. These take three to five days to grow.

Manna *Amaranthus hypochondriachus* These take 11 days to grow but were considered well worth waiting for by the Mexicans who referred to them as the 'Food of the Gods'.

Mung Beans *Phaseolus radiata* Used in many Chinese dishes; ready after four or five days.

Alfalfa or Lucerne

Puy Lentils and **Large Green Lentils** *Lens culinaris* Crunchy, fresh-tasting sprouts that take five days to grow.

Bean sprouts in a Chengdu market

57

'Trio'

Peas

Peas have been grown in S Europe and the Near East for thousands of years and pea seeds have been found in ancient settlements dating back to 5700 BC, which makes the cultivated pea as ancient a crop as wheat and barley. Peas are related to beans, groundnuts and clovers as well as to broad beans, chick peas and lentils. Peas can be eaten raw in salads, lightly boiled as fresh green peas when young, or, dried and made into a soup or potage. Mangetout, sugar peas or snow peas, in which the pods lack the stiff, parchment-like walls thus making the whole pod edible, are very good in salads either raw, if very young and sweet, or lightly cooked and added to the salad when cold. In parts of China the young green tops of the pea plants are picked and stir-fried as a vegetable.

PLANTING HELP Peas do best in a rich, light but moisture-retentive soil. They do not like very hot weather and do best in spring, cool summers or early autumn. Seeds should be sown in a V-shaped drill, in a single row, spaced 2in (5cm) apart and 1½in (4cm) deep. Newly planted seed and young plants will need to be protected from mice and pigeons, and the plants will benefit from support as soon as the tendrils appear, from

Peas growing in Rosmary Verey's potager

'Hurst Green Shaft'

'Waverex'   Mangetout pea 'Honey Pod'

much-branched sticks or supported netting. In dry weather, mulching and watering will improve the crop, especially from flowering onwards. In most varieties, continued picking of the young pods prolongs the cropping time.

'Honey Pod' A mangetout pea with long pods and round in cross section.

'Hurst Green Shaft' Has long straight pods and dark green peas. It has good yields and is resistant to pea wilt.

'Little Marvel' A popular, sweet, tender variety that matures in 62 days and has long pods.

'Little Marvel'

'Trio' Has extra sweet peas and matures in 74 days and produces pods in bunches of 3–5. The peas keep well.

'Waverex' A German variety that has short pods which are suitable for picking young as petit pois. It is tolerant of cool weather.

Broad Bean

Broad beans have been cultivated since Neolithic times; seeds have been found at digs in Jericho, Hungary and in Egypt dating back to 1800 BC. Broad beans are mentioned in Greek and Roman literature and primitive varieties with small black seeds have been excavated at Troy. The wild ancestor of the broad bean is not now known but it is assumed to have originated in the eastern Mediterranean region, where its near relative *Vicia narbonensis* is found. The broad bean is the hardiest of beans and the only one which can be sown in autumn for harvesting early the following summer. Most cultivars are large, upright annuals with hairy pods. The slightly flattened green or white beans are coarse and strong-flavoured when mature, but delicious when young. They can either be cooked and eaten cold with a dressing, or added raw to salads if they are young and sweet enough. (*See page 60 for Planting Help.*)

59

BEANS

PLANTING HELP   Broad beans prefer heavy well-manured soils and can either be sown in early winter (though they are vulnerable to slug and bird damage in the winter) or in very early spring on warmer soils. Alternatively, the seeds may be sown indoors in pots and planted out during a mild spell in early spring.

'Ite'   A prolific variety with small but well-flavoured beans, it matures in about 80 days under warm conditions.

'Red Epicure' This attractive variety has green pods but flowers and seeds that are deep red.

'The Sutton' The best variety for the smaller garden, being semi-dwarf but very prolific.

'Witkeim Major' A variety that has thick pods and green seeds and provides good yields from a spring sowing.

'Witkeim Major'

'Aquadulce Claudia'   An early long-podded hardy variety which is suitable for autumn sowing.

'Red Epicure'

'Red Epicure'

Broad beans in a Bolivian market

Dwarf broad bean 'The Sutton'

'Aquadulce Claudia' outgrowing its frame

Dwarf broad bean 'Ite'

Ripe soy beans

Soy Bean

Soy beans were probably first cultivated in NE China in the 11th century BC and thoughout Asia by the 3rd century BC. They were introduced into Europe from Japan in the 17th century but never became popular. Long valued in the East for their protein and oil, varieties have been selected to produce larger seeds for increased oil content and reduced protein content, non-climbing habit and non-shattering seed pods. Soy beans can be cooked and eaten as a high protein vegetable (especially good for vegetarians), or they can be added to a bean salad, or sprouted and added to raw salads or stir-fries (*see page 56*).

PLANTING HELP   Soy beans are tropical plants and grow well in climates with hot humid summers. In North America they take a minimum of 75 days to reach harvesting stage, and so should be sown about three months before the first frost of autumn. Quick-maturing modern varieties are also adapted to flowering and fruiting in the shortening days of July and August.

Soy beans with plastic mulch

'Ace'

Peppers

Peppers have been cultivated in Mexico since 5000 BC; it is probable that the hot types were grown rather than the large sweet peppers, although by 1500 AD when the first records of peppers being grown in Europe are found, all the main types were already established. Both the hot and mild peppers are derived from the species *Capsicum annuum*, which is native to Mexico and Central America. Two varieties are recognized: var. *annuum*, which includes all the cultivated types, and var. *minimum*, which includes the wild and weedy types.

Peppers of all kinds play an important role in the cuisines of numerous countries around the world, from the hot peppers of Indian and Mexican cooking, to the sweet peppers favoured by European and Mediterranean cuisines. Hot peppers, chilies and cayenne peppers are usually rather small and red when ripe and their degree of hotness depends on the presence of capsaicin; the amount varies according to yupe and is affected by the climate. Hot weather conditions produce hotter peppers and they become hotter and sweeter as they ripen, the seeds being hotter than the flesh. Hot peppers can be eaten raw (if you have a leather-lined mouth), pickled, cooked and added to stews, or dried and ground and used in a variety of dishes to add varying degrees of hotness, according to taste.

Sweet peppers, also known as pimentos and bell peppers, are popular in temperate countries and are widely grown in greenhouses in N Europe and in the open in S Europe, the Middle East and North America. The large hollow fruits are generally red when ripe but may be yellow; there are varieties which become blackish-purple as they mature. Sweet peppers can be eaten raw in salads or cooked, either stuffed and baked, or char-grilled on a barbecue, or added to stews or stir-fries.

'Ace'   Sweet pepper with large, green, quick-maturing fruit; suitable for a greenhouse in Britain, maturing in about 60 days in North America

'Albino'   A variety with upright, pointed fruit which ripens from white streaked purple to red on a very dwarf bush.

'Canapé'   Bred especially for cool climates, this will fruit outdoors in England in a sheltered garden or in an unheated frame, maturing in about 60 days. Green fruit turns red as it ripens.

'Italian Sweet'   The long fruits ripen red and are generally sweet rather than hot and are often used in pickled antipasto salads.

'Key Largo'   This variety has long fruit, tapering from a wide base with irregular grooves. The fruit is yellow green to orange red with thick, sweet flesh and more flavour than the large bell types.

'Long Sweet Banana'   These long, pale yellow peppers are not hot and ripen to red. A similar hot variety is known as Hungarian Yellow Wax.

'Perfection'   A true pimento with smooth, heart-shaped fruit, dark green ripening to red, maturing in 65–80 days in North America. The fruits are sweet with a strong flavour and commonly preserved by canning.

'Canapé'

PEPPERS

'Perfection'

'Santa Fe Grande'

'Long Sweet Banana'

'Key Largo'

'Purple Belle'

'Albino'

'Italian Sweet'

'Italian Sweet'

Pepper specimens from Malawi where they grow well outdoors

'Hot Gold Spike'

'Cayenne'

'Serrano'

'Red Chilli'

Pepper specimens from our cool greenhouse in Kent, England

PEPPERS

'Golden Belle'

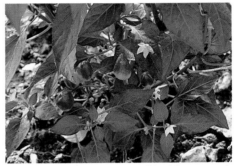

'Red Chilli'   'Albino' (*text page 62*)

PLANTING HELP   Peppers are fast-growing annuals and thrive in the drier parts of the tropics and in warmer weather. In temperate climates seed should be sown under glass in spring; the young plants can be put into growbags when they are about 3in (8cm) tall. They should be kept as warm as possible until hot weather arrives and then transferred to a sheltered place outside. Alternatively, young plants can be kept in pots until they are about 4¼in (11cm) tall and then hardened off and planted into frames in late June. Feeding is beneficial for building up a good-sized plant but it may be reduced when fruiting begins. Botrytis can be a problem in greenhouses and in wet seasons in the tropics, so good air circulation is needed to counteract this problem.

'Hot Gold Spike'   This yellow-fruited variety, commonly grown in the southwestern United States, is very hot when mature.

'Red Chilli'   This form of hot pepper has large, long fruit of variable hotness, maturing green, at which stage it is commonly eaten, and ripening red. It is often grown for canning in California and New Mexico.

'Cayenne'   An ancient cultivar from the pre-Columbian period, which is now mainly grown in Asia. The pods are long, slender and curved, ripening bright red and very hot. When dried and powdered this and similar cultivars produce the well-known Cayenne pepper.

'Golden Belle', 'Belle'   Fruits are large, thick-walled, ripening to orange yellow and maturing in about 65 days in North America.

'Purple Belle'   A compact plant with short, square fruit, changing from green to purple and red, maturing in about 70 days in North America (*illustration page 62*).

'Santa Fe Grande'   The fruits of this pepper are pale yellowish green when mature but ripen to red (*illustration page 62*).

'Serrano'   This Mexican chilli is widely grown commercially and is either eaten green or preserved by canning. It is not difficult to grow in a greenhouse in cool climates and produces a prolific crop on tall, much-branched and distinctly hairy plants.

CUCUMBER

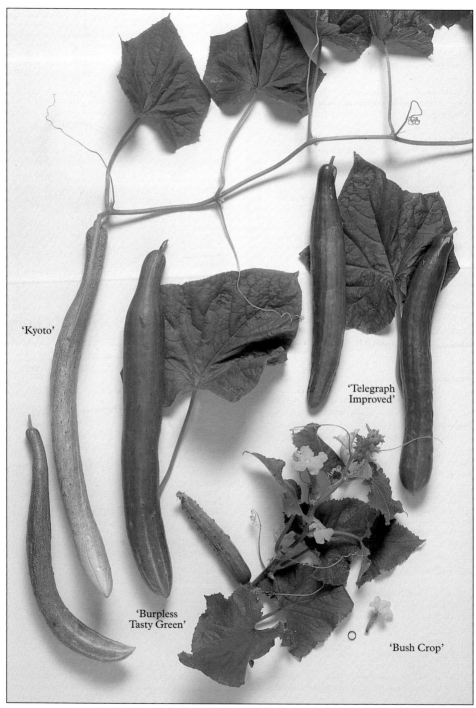

'Kyoto'

'Telegraph
Improved'

'Burpless
Tasty Green'

'Bush Crop'

Cucumber specimens from our cool greenhouse in Kent, England

Cucumber

The cucumber, like the melon, is a member of the genus *Cucumis*, which was probably cultivated in India from 1000 BC; it was also grown by the Greeks and spread west in early Classical times. It is believed to have originated in the wild in India, but nearly all other species of *Cucumis* are native to Africa. In India two forms of cucumber are grown: a green-fruited form with longitudinal white stripes; and a near white form which becomes rusty red at maturity. In Europe and North America most varieties have green skins with warts or soft spines on some of the hardier varieties.

Cucumbers are usually eaten raw as salad vegetables or made into pickles, but they are also excellent lightly cooked in butter and served with fish. In the E Mediterranean cucumbers are often mixed with yoghurt, garlic and mint to make a dip called tsaziki, they are also very popular in Scandinavia, where they are pickled and seved with pork.

PLANTING HELP   Cucumbers require a very rich soil with plenty of well-rotted manure and compost; they also need plenty of water and should never be allowed to dry out. In temperate climates plants from seed grown under glass produce the highest yields. Seed should be planted in winter and the young plants put in a raised bed or growbag in very early spring. A minimum temperature of 60°F (15°C) is needed for satisfactory growth; in unheated greenhouses leave planting until spring.

Train the climbing shoots on vertical wires and pinch out the apical shoot to encourage side shoots. Ridge cucumbers are hardier, and can usually be planted on ridges outside. The shoots can either be trained on horizontal wires or left to trail on the ground. It is important that the fruits of both greenhouse and ridge varieties are picked as soon as they are of edible size so that further fruits and flowers can be produced.

'Burpless Tasty Green'   An indoor or outdoor type that is not bitter.

'Bush Crop'   A short-growing, ridge or outdoor type, with slightly prickly fruit. Very good for growing in pots or growbags in a confined space.

'Chinese Long Green'   A hardy outdoor type and a robust climber, with long fruit.

'Kyoto'   A strongly climbing variety with narrow friuts up to 2ft (60cm) long. Suitable for outdoors or in the greenhouse.

'Chinese Long Green'

'Surprise'

'Surprise'   A smooth-skinned cucumber suitable for growing outdoors in southern Britain.

'Telegraph Improved'   Long, slender, dark green fruits and not bitter if the male flowers are removed to prevent pollination. Suitable for both greenhouse and outdoors in a sheltered place.

Courgette or Zucchini

The immature fruits of the vegetable marrow known as zucchini in Italian and courgette in French, together with pumpkin and squash, belong to the genus *Cucurbita* which contains 27 species of vigorous trailing and climbing annuals and perennials from North and South America. The cultivation of a number of the species dates back to pre-Columbian times when the native American diet was based on maize, beans and cucurbits. The genus includes a large number of very oddly shaped fruits known as gourds, pumpkins, squashes and vegetable marrows. Courgettes, cultivars of *Cucurbita pepo*, were introduced into Europe in the 16th century from their native North America. They have long or round fruits of various colours which are excellent to eat either raw, if young and sweet enough, or lightly boiled or steamed as a vegetable or stuffed

and baked. The young leaves and mature male flowers can also be eaten: the open flowers cooked in batter and the leaves cooked as greens. The bush kinds do not make long trailing branches and are therefore more suitable for small gardens or intensive cropping.

PLANTING HELP   Courgettes are voracious feeders and require plenty of manure to be dug into the soil. Strong supports for trailing varieties should be positioned prior to planting so that nearby plants are not smothered. The plants may also be set on top of the compost heap. Water regularly to ensure vigorous growth, especially from flowering until ripening of the fruits. Seed should be sown either individually or in a seed tray in spring under glass or *in situ* in spring once the danger of frost damage has passed. Seedlings are ready for planting out once they have developed four to six mature leaves. The young leaves, male flowers and first baby fruits are all delicious to eat and can be picked within two months of planting out.

'Burpee Golden', 'Golden Zucchini'   A bush variety with deeply lobed leaves, which can mature in North America in about 54 days. We have found this very drought tolerant.

'Tiger Cross'   A bush variety for use either as a marrow or as a courgette when young. Dark green mottled with cream, it is resistant to cucumber mosaic virus. (*not illustrated*).

'White Lebanese'   An old variety with very pale green fruit which is widely grown in Europe, the Middle East and Mexico. It takes 45–55 days to mature in North America.

'White Lebanese'

'Burpee Golden'

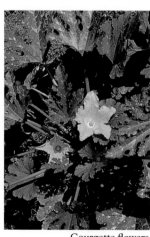

Courgette flowers

A greengrocer's wares, Lake Dal, Kashmir

'Gardener's Delight'

grow in profusion and are about ½in (1.5cm) across. This last group is generally sweeter and has more flavour than the large-fruited or medium-sized varieties. Other varieties have fruits that are elongated, plum-shaped and square, and these are used for canning.

PLANTING HELP   Tomatoes do best in a hot climate, with plenty of water while the plant is growing, and dry, sunny conditions while the fruits are ripening. They need fertile, well-drained, moisture-retentive soil and will also grow well in bags of peat or peat-like composts as long as they are correctly fed. In climates which have spring frosts, tomato seed should be sown indoors in heat and the plants grown on individually in pots before planting out in early summer when all danger of frost is over. This will usually be six to eight weeks after sowing and the first flower buds should be just opening. Tomato plants can also be grown in a greenhouse but the flavour of the fruit is much better when grown outside, provided that they ripen properly. The advantages of greenhouse cultivation are earlier and heavier crops, a longer period of fruit production in autumn and a wider choice of suitable varieties.

Bush varieties need no training but tall varieties will need staking and the side shoots need pinching out as they form. Tomatoes are prone to a number of pests and diseases, such as blossom end rot, which can be caused by too little or too much water; mosaic virus, which can be spread by aphids or even by being handled by a cigarette smoker; and green fly, white fly and red spider, which are serious in a greenhouse and are best controlled by regular, frequent spraying with soap.

'Gardener's Delight'   A tall, easy to grow plant. It has small fruit with an excellent flavour.

'Tigerella'

'Tigerella'   A tall-growing plant with medium-sized fruit. For growing indoors or outdoors.

Tomato

The tomato is one of about ten species of the genus *Lycopersicum*, all of which are native to W South America. They are all short-lived perennials that can be grown as annuals. Tomatoes were probably brought to Europe soon after the conquest of Mexico by Cortés in 1523, and were regarded with considerable suspicion, as most of the fruits of *solanums* (to which the tomato and the potato are related) were known to be poisonous.

Most tomato varieties belong to three main groups and there are also several odd varieties of lesser importance. The first group is the large-fruited Beef tomatoes which are often lobed and have fruits 4in (10cm) across. The second group is the medium-sized, round-fruited varieties which have fruits about 2in (5cm) across. The third group is the small-fruited Cherry tomatoes which

'Gardener's Delight' grown outside in Kent

Detail of flowers

'Sweet 100'

Dwarf tomato 'Red Robin'

'Beefsteak', 'Crimson'   A tall-growing plant with large fruit, ripening after 80–90 days in North America.

'Blizzard'   This variety is best grown under cover in Britain but tends to suffer from blossom end rot.

'Counter'   This variety is best grown under cover in Britain but tends to suffer from blossom end rot.

'Dombito'   This makes plants of intermediate height and is best grown under cover in Britain. It has large fruit and is thick-walled.

'Eurocross'   This has tall plants and medium-sized fruit and in Britain is best grown under cover with heat. It has good resistance to greenback and has a high yield but the flavour is rather poor and it tends to suffer from blossom end rot.

'Shirley'   A compact, early maturing plant that has good disease resistance and can be grown under glass.

'Moneymaker'   A tall-growing variety with medium-sized fruits, good for indoor and outdoor use. Very good flavour, especially when grown under cover, and it is not susceptible to blossom end rot.

'Red Robin'   A very dwarf plant with small fruit suitable for growing in in pots or window boxes.

'Sioux'   A tall-growing plant with medium-sized fruit that is good for indoor or outdoor use. It is not acid and has deep red fruit ripening after 70 days. It does tend to get blossom end rot.

'Striped Cavern'   A tall-growing variety with striped fruit which are ideal in size and shape for stuffing. It can be grown indoors or out but does get blossom end rot.

'Super Roma'   A pear-shaped tomato used for making paste, but with little flavour.

'Sweet 100'   A tall-growing plant with very small but prolific fruit and a good flavour, especially if grown outdoors. Suitable for growing either indoors or out.

TOMATOES

'Striped Cavern'

'Beefsteak'

'Sioux'

'Blizzard'

'Dombito'

'Shirley'

'Super Roma'

'Counter'

'Moneymaker'

'Eurocross'

Tomato specimens from Sellindge, Kent, England

TOMATOES

'Green Grape' photographed by Leslie Land

'Brandywine' An old Amish variety dating from 1885. It is tall-growing with large, dark reddish pink fruits and a wonderful flavour described as 'tomato heaven'. It is somewhat susceptible to disease.

'Green Grape' A new variety of Cherry tomato that makes a small bush which has quite large fruits with a wonderful flavour. When ripe the tomatoes are bright green inside.

'Ruffled Yellow' This variety has unusually shaped fruits that are rather hollow and suitable for stuffing.

'Yellow Perfection'

'Yellow Perfection' A tall-growing variety with medium-sized yellow fruits and a very good strong flavour; can be grown indoors or out.

'Zapotec Ribbed' A large-fruited, scarlet, ribbed variety grown by the Zapotecs in southern Mexico.

'Yellow Perfection'

'Zapotec Ribbed'

TOMATOES

'Brandywine' photographed by Leslie Land in Maine

'Ruffled Yellow' photographed by Leslie Land in Maine

Parsley

A stout hardy perennial, *Petroselinum crispum* probably originating in S Europe. Although not known as a wild plant, parsley is now commonly found naturalized in almost all temperate regions. For centuries parsley has been a universally favourite herb. It was known to the Greeks and the Romans and used medicinally by them. It was also thought to aid digestion, relieve flatulence, soothe bruises and toothache.

Flat-leaved parsley

However, it has probably been most highly valued for culinary uses, as it is rich in vitamin C, iron, magnesium and other vitamins and minerals. Although commonly used as a garnish, it can be used much more liberally in the cooking process itself. In Europe it is included in most herb mixtures and *bouquets garnis* as well as being added to soups, salads, casseroles and fish dishes. It can also be made into parsley sauce for cold lamb. Three forms of parsley are eaten: Crisped-leaf parsley, Flat-leaved parsley and Hamburg parsley in which the swollen roots are eaten as well as the flat leaves. The leaves of flat-leaved parsley are the main constituent of green salads in some countries. The roots of Hamburg parsley are eaten cooked and have a slightly sweet, nutty flavour – a cross between a delicate parsnip and a carrot. It is a traditional ingredient of a number of Polish, Croatian and Bulgarian dishes.

PLANTING HELP   Sow seed either in boxes or *in situ*, in spring for use in summer, or in summer for plants that will survive the winter and do well the following spring. Germination can be erratic and slow, so soak the seeds overnight before sowing. Flat-leaved parsley is easier to grow than the Crisped-leaf kinds and has a slightly stronger flavour. Hamburg parsley needs a growing season of at least three months in deep, well-tilled soil. The plants can either be planted close and harvested when young and small or they can be spaced about 6in (15cm) apart and allowed to grow until the winter. Beware of carrot fly infecting your parsley as it can result in poor growth, and check that slugs don't attack the roots, particularly of Hamburg parsley, and eat away the soft outer layer and so making the skin brown rather than white.

'Clivi'   A dwarf variety with basal leaves that do not go yellow when they get old.

'Green Velvet'   A close relative of 'Marshall's Moss Curled', it is said to have a piquant flavour.

'Hamburg'   A very ancient variety with edible roots tapering from a wide top, rather like small parsnips.

'Marshall's Moss Curled'   A very vigorous variety, probably the best for overwintering.

'Paramount Imperial Curled'   A dark green variety with tightly curled leaves.

Flat-leaved, Plain-leaved or **Italian Parsley**
This is also known as Sheep's parsley or Common parsley, and is the variety used in SE Europe and Asia. It has a stronger flavour than the curled varieties and is commonly used in Italian cooking.

Warning: Beware of eating wild parsley found in roadside ditches or damp woods; it could be the very poisonous Hemlock Water Dropwort *Oenanthe crocata*, which looks very similar to Plain-leaved parsley and can only be differentiated by its characteristic smell of angelica. If in any doubt do not eat it.

Coriander or Cilantro

The bright green leaves of *Coriandrum sativum* look similar to Broad-leaved parsley but the flavour is quite distinctively different. Coriander is an erect, aromatic annual, native to S Europe but now found widely distributed in many parts of Europe, Asia and North and South America. It grows wild in waste places and is also widely cultivated all over the world for use as a culinary herb and spice. Coriander seed has been used since ancient times for its flavour in cooking and medicinally to ease flatulence and in ointments for rheumatism and arthritis. It is an important ingredient of curry powders and spice mixtures and is very popular in Indian and Thai cooking. Coriander is also used to flavour frankfurters,

Coriander

PARSLEY & CORIANDER

'Marshall's Moss Curled'

'Paramount Imperial Curled'

'Green Velvet'

Flat-leaved parsley

'Clivi'

'Hamburg'

Parsley specimens from Sellindge, Kent

cakes, puddings, sweets and drinks. Fresh leaves are common in Egyptian, Georgian and Peruvian dishes, and pork cooked with coriander seeds is a favourite Greek dish. Fresh coriander is now a very popular addition to a variety of salads, contributing a delicious tangy, spicy flavour, particularly to milder green leaves.

PLANTING HELP   To grow coriander in a herb garden sow the seeds in early spring or autumn in light, fertile soil in a sunny position and, to ensure a continuous supply, make successive sowings. It flourishes best in cool spring weather and runs to seed very quickly in hot summers. Alternatively, sow seeds indoors in early spring or late summer, like cress. Leaves can be cut once they have reached 1–6in (2.5–15cm) and several cuts can be made from one sowing. Once the plants run to seed, its flavour deteriorates and plants should be uprooted.

Lemon Thyme

Thyme

Garden or Common thyme is a low, spreading evergreen shrub and has been used for centuries medicinally and cosmetically because of its antiseptic and aromatic qualities. The Egyptians incorporated thyme into their embalming ointments and the nobility in medieval times carried posies which included thyme, to ward off germs. Gargles, toothpaste, soaps and pot pourris are scented with thyme, and oil of thyme is used in aromatherapy and as a rub for rheumatism. Dried thyme is an essential culinary herb, being one of the main constituents of *bouquets garnis*, and is used in a wide range of meat, fish and vegetable dishes. Fresh thyme is delicious sprinkled on salads, grilled meat or fish and is also used to flavour oils and vinegars.

Thymus × citriodorus 'Silver Queen'

PLANTING HELP   Garden thyme can be raised from softwood cuttings taken in spring and rooted in compost. Keep the plants well trimmed and renew every three years.

Garden Thyme, Common Thyme *Thymus vulgaris*   An aromatic plant with tiny, slightly hairy leaves and numerous pale mauve flowers. Both leaves and flowers can be added to salads or dried for winter use.

Lemon Thyme *Thymus × citriodorus*   Has pink flowers and a strong lemon scent.

Thymus herba-barona   A variety which has pink flowers and is known as Caraway thyme. It is excellent in salads.

***Thymus × citriodorus* 'Silver Queen'**
This variety of Lemon Thyme has creamy silver variegations on the rather grey leaves, which have a pronounced lemon scent.

Thymus herba-barona

Savory

Winter Savory, a compact hardy evergreen perennial, and Summer Savory, an aromatic hardy annual, are both valued for their small, slightly spicy leaves and have been used for centuries as

Garden Thyme

culinary herbs. In the Middle Ages they were valued for their stimulating and soothing properties. Summer Savory is also known as 'the bean herb' because it enhances the flavour of many bean dishes without dominating them and aids the digestion of beans which give many people wind.

PLANTING HELP   Summer Savory is easy to grow from seed in a herb garden, needing rich light soil and plenty of sun. Sow seeds in spring and they should be ready for use in summer. Once it has flowered, pull up and dry (in bunches in the sun) and store for winter use. Winter Savory can be grown from seed in a similar way or it can be grown from root division or cuttings.

Summer Savory *Satureja hortensis*   Extensively cultivated all over the world as a pot herb but also sometimes found as an escape or wild on mountain slopes and moors. It has narrow, pointed, mid-green to red leaves and small white, pink or purple flowers.

Winter Savory *Satureja montana*   This has narrow oblong pointed leaves and bluish purple flowers. It has a sharper, spicier taste than Summer Savory.

Basil

Basil is a low-growing aromatic annual herb, native to Iran and India but now grown all over the world. It is rarely found in the wild except as an escape but is frequently cultivated in gardens. Basil is a very popular culinary herb, particularly on continental Europe. In France and Italy it is the main ingredient of *soupe au pistou* and *pesto* respectively, and fresh basil is particularly good sprinkled on tomatoes or *salade tricolor* – a combination of mozzarella, avocado and tomatoes.

Lemon Basil

PLANTING HELP   Basil is a tropical plant, easily grown from seed in a herb garden, window box or pot, but needs plenty of light, sun and warmth, so in a temperate climate keep it under glass and water sparingly and only in the morning. Sow seeds in late spring and once the plant is 6in (15cm) high, keep using the top leaves to encourage bushy growth.

Sweet Basil *Ocimum basilicum*   The fragrant alternate leaves are bright shiny green with distinctive veining. This is the variety most commonly found in shops to use in salads.

Lemon Basil *Ocimum* 'Citriodorum'   A small compact variety with a wonderful lemon scent.

Summer Savory

Winter Savory

Sweet Basil

Golden Marjoram

Marjoram or Oregano

The three main species of marjoram – Wild Marjoram, Sweet Marjoram and Pot Marjoram – and the numerous other cultivated varieties all have similar properties and uses, and a very long history of medicinal and culinary use. Marjoram has strong sedative and antiseptic powers which makes it good for herbal baths and pillows. Both Sweet Marjoram and Wild Marjoram are used for cooking, the former having the sweeter, more delicate flavour, and the latter the more spicy flavour, particularly if grown in a hot country. Pot marjoram is slightly bitter and not as sweet as the other two, although its flavour lasts longer in cooked dishes. It blends well with thyme and basil and is used to flavour pizzas, salami, sausages, stuffings and tomato dishes. The three main species of marjoram are hard to identify unless they are in flower; the majority of plants bought as Pot marjorams turn out to be forms of *Origanum vulgare*.

PLANTING HELP   Wild Marjoram can either be picked in the wild or grown in a herb garden. Marjorams are easy to grow from seed in any kind of soil but they need to be protected from the cold.

When putting out the seedlings make sure that you choose the driest, sunniest spot you can find.

Golden Marjoram *Origanum vulgare* 'Aureum' A variety of Wild Marjoram that has pretty golden leaves.

Compact Marjoram *Origanum vulgare* 'Compactum'   A low-growing variety of Wild Marjoram.

Compact Marjoram

Ginger Mint

Mint

There are many species and varieties of this popular aromatic herb which is used all over the world in cooking and in medicine. All the varieties listed here have similar properties to a greater or lesser degree. The medicinal properties of mints are numerous and well tested. They have antiseptic and anaesthetic properties and are an excellent tonic and aid to digestion. Mints are also popular culinary herbs, used to make jams, jellies and sauces to accompany meat and fish dishes. Fresh mint is used to make sauce for lamb, teas, cocktails and punches, and is delicious added to a variety of salads, particularly those involving tomatoes, cucumber or yoghurt.

PLANTING HELP   Mints are easily grown in a herb garden, rockery or pot. Propagate by taking cuttings in spring and autumn. They like damp, light soil with shade at the roots and sun on the foliage. Keep different varieties apart to prevent flavours mingling and watch out for rust fungus on the leaves. If this occurs dig up the affected mint immediately and burn it, then burn off the topsoil where the blight occurred to kill the spores. All mints are very invasive, so it is best to grow them in tubs or divided beds.

Apple Mint *Mentha rotundifolia*   Has large, round hairy leaves and is excellent in cooking and for flavouring summer drinks.

Ginger Mint *Mentha × gentilis*
Has golden variegated leaves and a slight ginger scent which makes an interesting addition to fresh salads.

Peppermint
Mentha × piperita
The oil is frequently used for flavouring sweets and cordials.; a hybrid of Spearmint and Watermint.

Spearmint
Mentha spicata
Introduced to Britain by the Romans and has remained a firm favourite for culinary use.

Spearmint

Apple Mint

Peppermint

Golden Sage (*left*) and Purple Sage

Sage

Garden Sage or Common Sage is an aromatic evergreen shrub that has long been used as a medicinal and culinary plant. Nowadays, it is principally used in cooking to flavour meat, stews, fish and soup. Because of its digestive properties it is frequently cooked with rich, fatty meat like pork or duck, and sage and onion stuffing is a well-known accompaniment for poultry. Fresh sage can be sprinkled sparingly on salads and on grilled fish or meat.

PLANTING HELP   Sage is easy to grow in the garden and likes ordinary dry soil and plenty of sun. Propagation is best from cuttings taken off well-established plants in spring. Woody stems should be cut back in early spring to encourage bushy growth and even though it is quite hardy, it should be mulched with sand in winter to encourage the shoots to root at the base. Plants may be replaced every four or five years if they become very woody.

Golden Sage *Salvia officinalis* 'Icterina'
A small plant with green and gold variegated leaves that can be used in salads.

Purple or **Red Sage** *Salvia officinalis* 'Purpurascens'   This has purplish red leaves and bright blue flowers. It can be used in salads or as an excellent gargle.

Fennel

Fennel is a stout perennial found naturalized in most temperate countries and cultivated almost worldwide. It has been cultivated as a culinary and medicinal herb since ancient times and several different varieties have been developed. The swollen bulbous fennel, known as Florence fennel or Sweet fennel, is best for salads. It was introduced to England in the 18th century from Italy, where it is a popular vegetable eaten raw with cheese, or braised. In cooking the sweet aniseed flavour of fennel leaves or seeds is delicious in a sauce or stuffing and counteracts the oiliness of some fish. It is used in marinades for pork and veal as well as in soups and salads. Medicinally, fennel is a marvellous aid to digestion and is useful in the treatment of toothache, earache, headaches, coughs and asthma.

PLANTING HELP   Leaf fennel can be grown easily in the garden or in a window box by sowing seeds in early spring or propagating by root division in spring. It likes well-drained loamy soil and a sunny position. Cut the green leaves when the plant begins flowering in summer. To grow good bulbs is difficult; the plants should be planted in deep rich soil, kept very well watered and grown as fast as possible, avoiding any disturbance to the roots when thinning plants to about 1ft (30cm) apart. Sow seeds in summer for a winter crop.

Bronze Fennel *Foeniculum vulgare*
'Purpurascens' A popular form with
bronze purplish tinged foliage that
looks very pretty in a herb garden or
herbaceous border.

Fennel *Foeniculum vulgare*
The fine soft green leaves
become grey green in autumn.

Florence Fennel
Foeniculum vulgare var.
dulce This has thick basal stalks which, when
young, can be eaten like celery with cheese, or
finely chopped and added to salads or they can be
boiled, braised or baked as a delicious vegetable.

Bronze Fennel

Dill

An aromatic annual, *Anethum graveolens* is now
commonly cultivated in many parts of the world.
Dill is found wild along roadsides and in waste
places in southern Europe and is easily recognized
by its thin, feathery blue green leaves, rather like
fennel but more luxuriant. It is now mostly
cultivated for culinary purposes, although it is still
the principal ingredient in infant gripe water
which is used to soothe babies' indigestion. It was
mentioned in Egyptian papyri and was used in the
Middle Ages as a medicinal as well as culinary
herb. Dill is considered of premier importance in
the preparation of fish dishes such as
Scandinavian cured salmon, gravadlax. As the
leaves lose their flavour when cooked for any
length of time, it is best to use them raw or add
them to a cooked sauce only minutes before
serving.

PLANTING HELP Dill can be cultivated in a
herb garden by sowing seeds from summer to
spring in any kind of soil as long as it is kept moist
and well weeded. The leaves can be cut at any
time, but are best just before flowering.

Dill

Good-sized bulbs of fennel

Bronze Fennel

Fennel

Nasturtiums and marigolds at Hollington's herb garden

Flowers for Salads

The centuries-old tradition of using both wild and cultivated flowers in cooking, principally in salads, has been revived recently. The great advantages of using flowers in salads is that they add additional and unusual flavours, and they also transform the appearance of the salad with their attractive shapes and colours.

While the use of certain flowers in cooking dates back to Classical times (the Greeks and Romans regularly used pinks, carnation and rose petals), other commonly grown ornamental flowers have only recently been used in Western cuisine for their interesting flavours. Other cultures, however, have eaten flowers as part of their diet for a long time; for example, day lilies have always been eaten by the Chinese but are only just becoming fashionable in Europe and North America. Use young flowers or those in bud, because once they are fully out they are past their best. Pick them early in the day when the morning dew has dried and, if necessary, wash gently in cold water and pat dry with a paper towel. Care is needed as flowers bruise easily. It is best to add flowers after the dressing so that they retain their freshness. There are some cooked dishes, too, which benefit enormously from the addition of flowers; meadowsweet fritters and bacon fried with dandelion flowers are examples. The flowery fragrance of elderflowers is an excellent addition to gooseberry ice cream. A note of caution. Some plants in the garden have toxic flowers so don't pick and eat flowers that you don't recognize, and also be wary of picking wild flowers that may have been sprayed or polluted.

Chrysanthemums

Chrysanthemum

Chrysanthemums have been cultivated by the Chinese since 500 BC and were taken to Japan in AD 800 where they have been a popular and important ingredient in Oriental cuisine. Although introduced earlier, *Dendranthema* cultivars became popular in Europe when Robert Fortune brought back the autumn-flowering varieties from China in 1843. Special varieties of chrysanthemum are used by the Japanese and Chinese but almost any kind of chrysanthemum grown in the garden can be added to salads. After picking the flowers, blanch the petals by dipping the flower heads in boiling water for a few seconds and then pluck off the petals and sprinkle them onto the salad. The Japenese eat the leaves deep-fried in tempura.

PLANTING HELP   Chrysanthemums grow easily in ordinary garden soil, particularly if they have a bit of sun and moderate watering. They are usually grown from cuttings taken in the spring or autumn and rooted in sandy soil.

Geranium

Geraniums (*Pelargoniums*) originate in South Africa and were brought to Europe in the 17th century, and became very fashionable in Victorian greenhouses. Both the leaves and flowers are edible and there is an enormous variety of colours and flavours to choose from; some are much more strongly flavoured than others, so experiment to find out which ones you prefer. Generally speaking however, the leaves should be used more sparingly than the flowers.

PLANTING HELP   Some varieties can be grown from seed planted indoors in early spring and bedded out in the garden when all risk of frost has gone. The scented varieties need to be grown from cuttings taken from the mature plants in autumn and kept frost-free over the winter months.

Geranium
'Graveolens'

Pot Marigold

The pretty annual marigold *Calendula officinalis*, related to the chrysanthemum, daisy and dandelion, is native to Europe and Asia, and has been used for centuries medicinally, cosmetically and in cooking. In the Middle Ages marigold was used to relieve internal problems as well as inflammation of the eyes, wounds, burns, bruises, eczema and acne. It was cultivated in kitchen gardens, and the flowers, which contain the colouring called calendulin, were used to dye butter and cheese yellow, as well as being added fresh to salads. Marigold petals are also used as a saffron substitute though they have a different flavour.

PLANTING HELP   Marigolds will grow in any soil in a sunny position. Sow seeds in spring, and once the plants are established, keep picking the flowers and dead leaves to prolong the flowering. Cut the flowers about mid-morning before they have fully opened out and use them fresh where possible, or dry them in a well-aired, shady place and store for future use.

Pot marigold

Nasturtiums and herbs in the potager at Ballymaloe Cookery School, Shanagarry, Cork, Ireland

Nasturtium

An annual native of Peru that was introduced into Europe at the end of the 16th century, *Tropaeolum majus* has a long history of medicinal, cosmetic and culinary use. The nasturtium's high vitamin C content made it an effective remedy for scurvy and it was used as a general tonic for the digestion. The flowers, leaves and seeds have a pungent peppery taste and make a decorative, tangy addition to salads. The seeds can also be pickled and used as a substitute for capers.

PLANTING HELP   Nasturtiums will thrive in poor soil and dry conditions and can be grown from seed in the garden or in a window box or on a balcony. They will self-seed prolifically once they have taken hold, but they are not frost hardy, indeed, they are one of the first plants in the garden to be killed by frost.

Nasturtiums

Primrose

Hollyhocks in the reconstruction of Clusius' original 16th-century herb garden in Leiden, Holland

Primrose

A perennial that grows wild in woods, hedgerows and pastures as well as being grown in gardens, *Primula vulgaris* has very pretty yellow flowers that can be added whole to salads and were valued in the past for their medicinal properties.

PLANTING HELP   Primroses like humus-rich soil in a slightly shaded position; they can be sown from seed in autumn in a shaded frame and planted out the following spring or autumn. Every three years the mature plants can be divided.

Hollyhock

Introduced to Europe in the 16th century, possibly from China, *Althaea rosea* is now widely naturalized and cultivated in gardens or found growing as garden escapes. As well as being grown for their ornamental value, hollyhocks were also used medicinally as a substitute for marsh mallow, having similar soothing and diuretic properties, and the purple-flowered varieties were used for colouring wine. Hollyhock flowers and cooked buds can be added to salads and are particularly good with lettuce.

PLANTING HELP   Hollyhocks like rich moist soil and can easily be grown from seed. Tall varieties may need staking; in very cold areas they may need to overwinter in frames then be planted out in spring.

Hollyhock

87

A field of sunflowers in Gascony

Sunflower

The sunflower *Helianthus annuus* is a large annual native to North and Central America, which was introduced into Europe in the 16th century. It is now widely cultivated as an economic crop as well as for its ornamental value. Not only do the seeds yield an oil that is excellent for cooking, but they can also be eaten raw or roasted in salads and cereals. The young flower buds can be lightly boiled and eaten whole; some say they taste like asparagus, others have compared their flavour to Jerusalem artichokes. The petals, at their best in July and August, can be eaten, either raw or cooked. When the seed heads droop, cut them off and leave to dry. When fully dried the seeds will easily fall out and they can then be stored in a dry, cool place until needed.

PLANTING HELP   Sunflowers can be grown easily in the garden. Sow seeds in boxes in spring and plant out in early summer, preferably in enriched soil but any soil will do as long as there is plenty of sun and light

Dandelion

The flowers of *Taraxacum officinale* have traditionally been used to make dandelion wine, but can also be added to salads for colour and flavour or fried with bacon.

PLANTING HELP   Dandelion is found growing wild and in gardens throughout the

Northern Hemisphere. Gather the flowers when they are young and tender for use in salads as they become bitter when they are older (*see page 19*).

Daisy

A perennial native to Europe and W Asia, *Bellis perennis* grows wild in abundance wherever there is grass. In times past daisies were considered to have numerous medicinal properties and are still used in homoeopathy. The little white flowers can be sprinkled whole onto salads and separate petals of the larger pink red or white cultivated varieties can be used too.

Daisy

PLANTING HELP   The cultivated daisies should be sown in early spring to flower the same year; though perennial, they are better treated as biennials, as by the third year, they lose their vigour. Remove the dead heads to prolong flowering. Lift and replant self-sown seedlings to avoid overcrowding.

Violet

A perennial found growing wild on hedgebanks and in open woods, *Viola odorata* is also cultivated in gardens. The sweet-smelling flowers have been used since ancient times to perfume confectionery, wine, cosmetics and medicines. Violets were also traditionally eaten raw with lettuce and onions and look very pretty sprinkled onto salads. Gather the flowers in spring for immediate use or dry them carefully in the shade to retain their colour and then store them in stoppered jars, away from the light, for future use.

PLANTING HELP   Violets can be grown easily in the garden either from seed or from last season's runners. Plant in moist, leafy, chalky soil in a shady spot and make sure they have plenty of moisture until firmly rooted.

Heartsease

An annual or short-lived perennial native to Europe and W Asia, the Wild pansy *Viola tricolor* is also found growing as a weed in other parts of the world. Its combination of violet, white and yellow flowers and its velvety texture make it a charming addition to any salad. Wild pansy can be collected from the wild or grown from seed in the garden. It likes good soil and light shade. Sow in spring for

autumn flowering and in autumn for spring flowering; every few years divide the plants. The flower petals of Garden Pansy *Viola wittrockiana* can also be eaten.

PLANTING HELP   Wild pansies are very easy to grow from seed in any soil, with a reasonable amount of sun. They will happily self-seed over the years.

Dandelion

Violet

Heartsease

Pinks

The carnation (*Dianthus*) was one of the earliest flowers to be cultivated in Britain for its decorative, culinary and medicinal properties. Its spicy, clove-like fragrance was used to flavour vinegars, ales, wines, sauces and salads. The petals were candied to decorate cakes and dried for use in pot pourris. The flowers can be added to salads to add pungency and colour.

PLANTING HELP   Various pinks are found as garden escapes or they can be grown easily from seed in the garden, particularly on rockeries, stone walls, paths or borders. Most varieties need well-drained soil and either full sun or partial shade.

Rocket

The versatile salad plant *Eruca sativa* has very pretty yellowish or cream flowers with deep violet veins. The flowers of rocket as well as the leaves can be added to mixed green salads to add colour and a distinctive spicy taste.

PLANTING HELP   Rocket can be grown from seed in any kind of soil, in a sunny position (*see page 18*).

Dianthus 'Cheddar Pink' with *Alchemilla mollis*

Hyssop

An aromatic perennial, *Hyssopus officinalis* has been used in Mediterranean countries since pre-Christian times for medicinal and culinary purposes. The strong aromatic odour of the flowers, leaves and young shoots makes it a delicious addition to salads, game soups and fruit pies, but it does need to be used sparingly.

PLANTING HELP   Hyssop is a fairly hardy plant and can be grown easily in an herb garden from cuttings, seeds or by root division. It prefers light, dry soil and a warm spot, but nevertheless should be kept well watered until established.

Chives

Although mostly grown for its leaves, the pretty pale mauve or pink flowers of *Allium schoenoprasum* can be added to salads to add colour as well as a mild onion flavour.

PLANTING HELP   Chives can be grown easily in an herb garden, window box or pot either from seed or by dividing old plants. They are happy in any kind of soil as long as they are given extra moisture in dry weather (*see page 44*).

Rocket

Borage

Hyssop

Chives

Borage

Since ancient times *Borago officinalis* has been regarded as having a wonderful effect on mind and body, and has been used medicinally and in the kitchen. The young leaves are cooked and eaten as a pot herb, shredded into salads, made into a refreshing drink with the addition of lemon and honey or added to Pimms for flavour and as garnish. The flowers are edible and were frequently candied and eaten as sweetmeats; they also look very pretty added to salads.

PLANTING HELP   Borage can either be found wild or grown from seed in a window box or herb garden. It prefers moist, fertile, loose, stony soil with some chalk and sand in it and will stand some frost. Borage seed germinates quickly and it easily reseeds itself, so you will find it coming up on the same spot year after year.

Rose

For centuries roses have been prized for their medicinal, cosmetic and culinary properties. In medieval times cakes, jams, wines and sweetmeats were flavoured with crushed rose petals and rose powder, while rose oil and water, and rose petals were used to perfume the body and sweeten the breath. Medicinally, roses were recommended for their astringent and tonic properties. The petals of any roses, whether wild or cultivated can be eaten in salads. Pick those with the most fragrance to flavour other salad leaves.

Roses

PLANTING HELP   Many types of roses are easily grown in the garden. Generally, they like deep rich soil and plenty of sun. Preferably pick petals and add to salads just before eating.

Lily

Lily is a name applied to a variety of flowers, many of which are not true lilies and some of which are not edible. However, all flowers of the genus *Lilium* are edible. Lily bulbs were eaten by the Romans and the tiger lily has long been popular in Chinese cooking, with the flower being used either fresh or dried for seasoning and the bulbs for pickling. Other varieties of bulb have been consumed by the Japanese for their sweet taste. Old varieties and newer hybrids can all be used, either fresh or dried, to add a delicate flavour to salads and other dishes.

PLANTING HELP   Lilies can be grown in the garden or in pots by planting bulbs in spring or autumn, with good drainage below the bulb and loose fertile soil above. They like their roots to be in the shade but their heads in the sun.

Day Lily

The Chinese and Japanese have long recognized the edible qualities of *Hemerocallis* flowers and, with the increasing interest in Pacific Rim cuisine, they have become popular in Europe and North America too. Whole flowers can be dipped in batter and lightly fried or used fresh in salads to add a crisp texture and delicate flavour. Flowers can also be dried and sealed in jars to last all year and revived by soaking in water.

Lilium auratum

PLANTING HELP   Gladioli, which come in a variety of colours and sizes, are grown from corms. They may be increased either from seed or from young corms around the parent plants. Flowers should be picked early in the morning, washed thoroughly, patted dry and kept in a plastic bag in the fridge until ready for use.

A field of Day lilies in the USA

Hemerocallis 'Cherry Ripe'

PLANTING HELP   Day lilies are hardy perennials. Plant the roots in ordinary soil, in spring or autumn, spacing them about 3ft (90cm) apart as they quickly develop into large clumps

Gladiolus

Gladiolus has long been admired for its beauty, which led 18th-century horticulturists to develop a huge range of hybrids and cultivars, in addition to the 150 or so species that already existed. Gladiolus flowers or petals are extremely pretty added to salads, or the whole flower can be used as a container for dips with chicken, prawn or tuna salads.

Gladiolus

Index

INDEX

INDEX